Bipolar Disorder

PROVEN SOLUTIONS *for* **IMMEDIATE HELP**

A GUIDE *for* THE NEWLY DIAGNOSED

Janelle M. Caponigro, MA, Erica H. Lee, MA,
Sheri L. Johnson, PhD, Ann M. Kring, PhD

"One of the most confusing—but ultimately liberating—steps for people with bipolar disorder is getting that initial diagnosis. Often frightening, upsetting, and filled with shame, you don't know what to expect or what to do. *Bipolar Disorder: A Guide for the Newly Diagnosed* by Caponigro, Lee, Johnson, and Kring fills this gap. This highly readable and accessible guide provides you with basic information on how to recognize the important symptoms of bipolar disorder; the essential role of medication and which psychological treatments can be helpful; and how to cope with family, friends, work, and on-going self-care. I know that this book will be invaluable for those coping and living with bipolar disorder and will give much needed hope and guidance. I strongly recommend this guide for those new to their diagnosis. In many ways, coming to terms with the illness and acquiring effective coping skills are part of that first step toward getting better, and that first step may prove to be the most important one.

> —Robert L. Leahy, PhD, author of *The Worry Cure* and
> *Beat the Blues Before They Beat You*

"This is a very readable and comprehensive book for someone adjusting to a diagnosis of bipolar disorder. The discussions of the social aspects of the process—for example, who to tell and what to say, or meeting with a therapist and building a treatment team—are particularly helpful. I highly recommend this book as a first step to fitting bipolar disorder into a full and satisfying life."

> —Greg Murray, professor and head of psychology at
> the Swinburne University of Technology, Australia

"Bipolar disorder can be a debilitating illness that affects every aspect of life. Forewarned is forearmed, and this text provides invaluable information for people with bipolar disorder and the people who love them about what to expect from the illness and how to deal with it. The authors are among the most distinguished experts in the field. I strongly recommend this marvelous and totally accessible text."

—Steven Hollon, PhD, professor of psychology
at Vanderbilt University

"This is a very well written, accessible guide for someone recently diagnosed with bipolar disorder, or their friends and family. The key message is one of hope. People with bipolar disorder can find ways to understand and manage their bipolar experiences in ways that allow them to lead full and satisfying lives. This book outlines the key steps to learning how to do this and covers both medication and psychosocial approaches. The book includes case examples to bring the key messages to life, and signposts the reader to many other useful resources for more detailed information. I think this book would be useful for anyone looking for more information on how to best manage bipolar disorder."

—Fiona Lobban, PhD, DClinPsy, senior lecturer
in clinical psychology at the Spectrum Centre for
Mental Health Research at Lancaster University, UK

"Too often, the field struggles with what appear to be competing demands for a scientific basis versus clinical acumen or presence in the moment with each client. This book brings together evidence, experience, and empathy in an all-too-rare amalgam. I do not have a better word for it than 'wisdom.' Combining proven interventions and recent developments, this book fills a distinct and important role. I recommend it most highly."

> —Eric Youngstrom, PhD, professor of psychology and psychiatry and acting director at the Center for Excellence in Research and Treatment of Bipolar Disorder at the University of North Carolina at Chapel Hill.

GUIDES *for the*
NEWLY DIAGNOSED
Series

New Harbinger's Newly Diagnosed book series was created to help people who have recently been diagnosed with a mental health condition. We understand that receiving a diagnosis can bring up many questions. For example, whom should you tell about your diagnosis? What treatments are available? What are the best techniques for managing your symptoms? And how do you start building a support network?

Our goal is to offer user-friendly resources that provide answers to these common questions, as well as evidence-based strategies to help you better cope with and manage your condition so you can get back to living a more balanced life.

Visit www.newharbinger.com for
more books in this series.

Bipolar
Disorder

A GUIDE *for*
THE NEWLY
DIAGNOSED

Janelle M. Caponigro, MA, Erica H. Lee, MA,
Sheri L. Johnson, PhD, Ann M. Kring, PhD

New Harbinger Publications, Inc.

Publisher's Note

Care has been taken to confirm the accuracy of the information presented and to describe generally accepted practices. However, the authors, editors, and publisher are not responsible for errors or omissions or for any consequences from application of the information in this book and make no warranty, express or implied, with respect to the contents of the publication.

The authors, editors, and publisher have exerted every effort to ensure that any drug selection and dosage set forth in this text are in accordance with current recommendations and practice at the time of publication. However, in view of ongoing research, changes in government regulations, and the constant flow of information relating to drug therapy and drug reactions, the reader is urged to check the package insert for each drug and consult with their health care provider for any change in indications and dosage and for added warnings and precautions. This is particularly important when the recommended agent is a new or infrequently employed drug.

Some drugs and medical devices presented in this publication may have Food and Drug Administration (FDA) clearance for limited use in restricted research settings. It is the responsibility of the health care provider to ascertain the FDA status of each drug or device planned for use in their clinical practice.

Distributed in Canada by Raincoast Books

Copyright © 2012 by Janelle M. Caponigro, Erica H. Lee, Sheri L. Johnson, & Ann M. Kring,
New Harbinger Publications, Inc.
5674 Shattuck Avenue
Oakland, CA 94609
www.newharbinger.com

Cover design by Amy Shoup; Text design by Michele Waters-Kermes;
Acquired by Melissa Kirk; Edited by Jasmine Star

Library of Congress Cataloging-in-Publication Data

Bipolar disorder : a guide for the newly diagnosed / Janelle M. Caponigro ... [et al.].
 p. cm. -- (The New Harbinger guides for the newly diagnosed series)
 Summary: "Bipolar Disorder: A Guide for the Newly Diagnosed is a pocket guide to symptom management, treatments, medications, and more for people who have been recently diagnosed with bipolar disorder. Includes guidance for processing the diagnosis, sharing it with family and friends, and finding experts who can help get symptoms under control"-- Provided by publisher.
 Includes bibliographical references.
 ISBN 978-1-60882-181-5 (pbk.) -- ISBN 978-1-60882-182-2 (pdf e-book) -- ISBN 978-1-60882-183-9 (epub)
 1. Manic-depressive illness. 2. Manic-depressive illness--Diagnosis. 3. Manic-depressive illness--Treatment. I. Caponigro, Janelle M.
 RC516.B52228 2012
 616.89'5--dc23

                                   2012016989

Printed in the United States of America

14   13   12
10 9 8 7 6 5 4 3 2 1   First printing

CONTENTS

Introduction

Over the past decade, bipolar disorder, which is defined by symptoms of mania, has captured the public imagination and become the focus of many movies. Rates of diagnosis have soared, and Armani even markets a perfume named Mania. On the one hand, we've been given images of highly accomplished individuals who have this condition. Kay Redfield Jamison (1993) has described evidence that authors Ernest Hemingway and Charles Dickens, musician Robert Schumann, and artists Georgia O'Keeffe, Jackson Pollock, and Mark Rothko all had this disorder. On the other hand, all too often people with bipolar disorder struggle with sustaining jobs, relationships, and self-esteem due to mood episodes, and we are flooded with media images that portray the dark side of an uncontrolled, untreated illness. In the midst of these conflicting images, it can be hard to obtain carefully documented information about what the disorder really is and how to manage it well. Our goal is to provide this.

We strongly believe that there are reasons for hope. Many people with this condition learn to live full and satisfying lives, and most say that they wouldn't erase the disorder if they could do so. But we want to be more than just an optimistic voice. This book was written to help those with bipolar disorder begin to control the illness, rebuild parts of their lives that have been damaged, and sustain wellness. We see this book as a kind of tool kit: a survival guide offering key resources and strategies on the path to recovery.

We begin with the basics. For many people, mood episodes, hospitalizations, and encounters with doctors can go by in a confusing blur, so chapter 1 provides definitions of what doctors mean when they use terms like "bipolar disorder" and "mania." Because misdiagnosis can and does occur in this era of busy health care systems, we hope this helps you sort through some of the confusing terms and lingo. We also provide a snapshot of the biological roots of this condition.

With bipolar disorder, a key strategy is to find a good treatment team. In chapter 2, we provide an overview of that process. We discuss what types of providers to consider, note some sources for referrals, and discuss what to expect during initial sessions.

For most people with bipolar disorder, medications will be the mainstay of treatment. However, several different types of medications are used to treat bipolar disorder, and even within a given category of medication, there are many different options. In chapter 3, we explain the rationale guiding selection of medications and also provide an overview of the most common side effects. Our goal in this chapter is to help you understand that you have many different options so that you can be an active partner with your doctor in coming up with the best treatment plan.

Evidence based on studies of thousands of people with bipolar disorder has clearly shown that adding psychotherapy to medications can help people recover from mood episodes more quickly, maintain their periods of wellness, improve their social relationships, restore their work lives, and reduce their odds of hospitalization. Several different types of psychotherapy have been proven effective, and in chapter 4 we review the best of these.

Because bipolar disorder symptoms often come and go, most people want to know why their symptoms emerge at a given time. In chapter 5 we describe the most common triggers of depression and mania. By helping you consider when and how episodes might arise, we hope to enhance your sense that these episodes can be predictable and therefore controllable. Most importantly, being aware of triggers and early signs of relapse provides an opportunity to cope with those early warning signs. Evidence shows that this awareness helps people stay well, so we review a host of possible strategies in chapter 6.

Without a doubt, adjusting to the diagnosis is a difficult process, and one that is eased by the support of loved ones. Despite that, having bipolar disorder raises lots of questions about relationships. Who should know about your diagnosis and symptoms? How might you describe this condition to others? How do you identify people who can understand this experience? In chapter 7 we discuss some of the core issues in making sure that you're well

3

supported and understood as you gain better control over mood episodes.

In chapter 8, we end the book by describing some of the advantages that can come with this disorder, including evidence that mania is linked to creativity, drive, and many other positive traits.

It is our hope that this book provides a road map toward health. We've watched many people as they learned to manage their symptoms, achieved wellness, and built the lives they want to live. We hope this book points the way toward that path.

CHAPTER 1

UNDERSTANDING BIPOLAR DISORDER

We believe that the road to health means learning everything you can to help manage your symptoms of bipolar disorder. This book is designed to increase your understanding of bipolar disorder and teach you skills to prolong your periods of wellness. In this chapter, we'll share information about how doctors recognize and diagnose bipolar disorder, the biology of the illness, and other symptoms or disorders you may experience. We'll also dispel a few common myths about bipolar disorder. This chapter will provide key information and establish a common language that will come in handy throughout the rest of the book as we discuss treatment options, illness management, and tools to help provide relief.

Bipolar disorder is a biological illness that affects your ability to regulate your mood and leads to feelings of extreme happiness, intense sadness, or heightened irritability. It is considered an illness because, like other medical disorders such as heart disease or diabetes, it occurs after a biological change in your body, has well-described symptoms, and causes distress to people who have it.

The diagnosis of bipolar disorder is considered when a person has had at least one episode of mania or hypomania (a less intense form of mania). Many people with bipolar disorder also experience periods of depression, which is why the term "bipolar" is used. So there are two broad categories of bipolar symptoms: mania and depression.

The way people experience the symptoms of bipolar disorder is highly individualized. Your experience will have both similarities to and differences from the experience of others. However, one aspect is consistent: At some point, these symptoms cause distress or make it hard to function at work, school, or home, or with family and friends. Many people with bipolar disorder need professional help, such as seeing a psychiatrist or being temporarily hospitalized, in order to manage their symptoms, remain in good health, maintain their relationships, and enjoy a higher quality of life.

Certain symptoms tend to occur together, and when they do, mental health providers call this experience a *mood episode*. Symptoms that occur while feeling high, euphoric, or irritable are called *manic* or *hypomanic episodes*. Symptoms that occur when feeling down, blue, or emotionally empty are called *depressive episodes*. In the next section, we'll walk you through what experiences and symptoms form the criteria for a mood episode.

MANIC EPISODES

If you have a diagnosis of bipolar disorder, you've probably experienced times when you felt extremely good, energetic, or high. It's natural to feel great at certain times in life, like after receiving a promotion or hearing good news about a loved one. However, people with bipolar disorder may feel overly positive or find that their response to these types of events lasts for days longer than what other people might experience. And for people with bipolar disorder, sometimes these feelings of being on top of the world seem to come out of the blue. Others find themselves experiencing unusual and unexplained periods of irritability, argumentativeness, or impatience. For example, your conversations may involve complaints or hostile comments, and you may even find yourself arguing with strangers.

A manic episode is defined as a distinctly elevated or irritable mood in combination with three or more additional symptoms of mania (described below). These symptoms must last longer than one week. When the mood state is irritable rather than elevated, four or more additional symptoms of mania are required for the diagnosis.

Mania Symptoms

Mania refers to the high or elevated periods of bipolar disorder. It is defined by a shift in mood that involves feeling extremely good, excited, or euphoric, though a manic episode may also be characterized by feeling irritable, argumentative, or impatient. In

7

addition to these changes in mood, mania includes experiencing at least three or four of the symptoms described below:

INCREASED SELF-CONFIDENCE

Everyone has qualities that are unique to them and important, but during a manic episode you may believe in your abilities with more confidence than usual. This may include thinking you can do things that you may not be prepared or equipped to take on or offering tips on a topic you may know nothing about. Confidence is a good thing, but in mania your self-esteem may be too high, causing you to make inappropriate decisions. You may feel as though nothing is impossible and every problem has a solution. Doctors may refer to this symptom as *grandiose thinking.*

DECREASED NEED FOR SLEEP

Most people need a certain amount of sleep to feel rested. In a manic episode you may sleep much less than your normal amount but still feel rested and energized in the morning. For example, you may sleep three hours or stay up all night and still be ready to start your day with as much energy as if you'd slept nine hours.

TALKATIVENESS

Mania may cause you to talk faster and louder, or you might start conversations with strangers. You may feel frustrated when people ask you to repeat yourself. Sometimes a person is most aware of these changes because of what other people say. For example, others may tell you, "Slow down! I can't follow what you're saying." or "Hey! Can I get a word in here?" This behavior is often referred to as *pressured speech.*

RACING THOUGHTS

With racing thoughts, you feel like your thoughts are coming faster than you can put them into words. You may have several ideas at once, making it difficult to finish one thought before starting another, or you may feel that your thoughts are unorganized and difficult to make sense of. Sometimes this symptom is referred to as a *flight of ideas.*

DISTRACTIBILITY

During a manic episode everything seems interesting, which makes it difficult to focus or to pay attention to one thing at a time. You may be easily distracted by internal experiences (such as thoughts and ideas) or external events (whatever is going on around you). You may also find that you can't get through the morning paper or your favorite TV show because your mind keeps wandering off somewhere else. Distractibility can make it difficult to get things done at work, school, or home.

INCREASED GOAL-DIRECTED BEHAVIOR

In a manic episode you may find that you spend a lot of time planning or participating in multiple activities. For example, you may take on several new projects within a short time frame. Ambition is a good thing, but when you're feeling manic you may take on several projects without taking the steps necessary to set yourself up for success. You might skip getting educated on a certain topic, gaining work experience, saving money and budgeting, or finding the social support you need to accomplish your goals. For example, you might use all of your savings to start a law practice even though you don't have a law degree and never wanted to be a lawyer before.

PSYCHOMOTOR AGITATION

With mania, you may experience sensations of restlessness or the feeling that you can't sit still for a long period of time. You may feel like pacing around a room or continually wringing your hands even if you want to rest or sit down. This is termed *psychomotor agitation* because feelings of tension or restlessness can cause excessive physical activity.

EXCESSIVE INVOLVEMENT IN PLEASURABLE ACTIVITIES

In a manic episode you may participate in pleasurable activities that may not be safe or responsible, such as spending money excessively, engaging in risky sexual activity, or making decisions quickly without thinking through the consequences. For example, you may abruptly leave on a vacation without notifying your boss or spend a lot of money on things you can't afford. In the moment, these decisions may seem fun and exciting, but they often lead to negative consequences down the road.

HYPOMANIC EPISODES

Not all people who have bipolar disorder experience a manic episode. Some people experience fewer and less intense manic symptoms for a shorter amount of time. This is called *hypomania*. A hypomanic episode is defined as an abnormally high or irritable mood in combination with three or more symptoms of mania lasting at least four days. The key difference between hypomania and mania is that mania creates difficulties in a person's life, such as conflicts with employers or family members, reckless behaviors, or financial problems. Hypomania is less severe, and while it is clearly different from how you usually feel, you may not experience disruptions or problems in your daily life as a result of these symptoms. Another difference is the length of symptoms. By definition, manic episodes must last at least one week, whereas hypomanic episodes may be as brief as four days. Determining the difference between mania and hypomania can sometimes be challenging, since it may be difficult to remember the intensity of your symptoms and how long they lasted.

DEPRESSIVE EPISODES

The words "depression" and "depressed" are often used in the media and in everyday conversations. However, psychologists and physicians define a depressive episode as the presence of five or more symptoms of depression (described below) experienced most of the day nearly every day for at least two weeks. At least one of the five symptoms must be depressed mood or loss of interest or pleasure in activities (also known as *anhedonia*). Even though we often think of depression as feeling down or blue, you can meet the diagnosis for depression without feeling sad. In fact, people with bipolar disorder commonly don't experience sadness when depressed, but instead have a sense of emotional emptiness or indifference.

Depression Symptoms

The depressive symptoms of bipolar disorder are the same as those seen among people who experience depression without manic symptoms. When depressive symptoms occur in a person who has never experienced manic or hypomanic symptoms, it is called major depressive disorder or unipolar depression. However, when people with bipolar disorder experience depression, it usually occurs more often, arises more quickly, and is felt more intensely than unipolar depression. Therefore, it's important to educate yourself on how to recognize not only the highs of mania, but also the lows of depression. Depression is defined by a shift in mood that involves feelings of immense sadness, emptiness, or worthlessness. You may also lose interest in your usual activities or find that the things that usually make you feel good don't anymore, like going to the movies or spending time with friends and family. Depression also includes experiencing some of the symptoms described below.

CHANGES IN EATING HABITS

You may gain or lose more than 5 percent of your body weight in a month or experience an increase or decrease in appetite. For example, you may find that you're eating more than usual or that you never feel hungry and must force yourself to eat because you know your body needs food.

CHANGES IN SLEEP

You may experience *insomnia*, meaning you have trouble falling asleep or staying asleep. You may also find yourself having difficulty getting out of bed in the morning or waking up early in the morning and being unable to fall back asleep. Alternatively, you may sleep more than usual which is called *hypersomnia*.

PSYCHOMOTOR AGITATION OR SLOWING

You may feel agitated, restless, or unable to sit still, as in mania. But you could also experience the opposite. You could feel extremely slowed down in your thinking, movements, or speech. Sometimes this is called *psychomotor retardation.*

FATIGUE OR LACK OF ENERGY

You may feel exhausted, like all the energy has been drained from your body. As a result, you may have difficulty doing things that are usually easy for you or accomplishing things that normally don't require much effort.

FEELINGS OF WORTHLESSNESS OR GUILT

You may feel like you're inferior or as though you're responsible for bad things that happen that might have nothing to do with you. You may also find yourself feeling guilty about past events.

DISTRACTIBILITY OR INDECISIVENESS

You may have a hard time getting work done, remembering things, or making decisions. Paying attention may feel extremely difficult.

SUICIDALITY

You may feel as though your symptoms of mania or depression will last forever and that there is no hope. Thinking about death, dying, or suicide is a very common experience for people with bipolar disorder. It has been estimated that about one-third of people with this illness attempt to commit suicide at some point in their lifetime (Chen and Dilsaver 1996). There are levels of severity of suicidal thinking. Every level is a sign of serious pain, but thinking about death or wanting to die doesn't mean that a person will commit suicide. It is important to talk openly about these thoughts and experiences with your treatment providers so they can offer you help and support. Mental health professionals usually start developing a safety plan to intervene against a possible suicide attempt if you start thinking about *how* you would take your own life.

PERSONAL EXPERIENCES WITH MOOD EPISODES

Here are two stories of people who have experienced mood episodes like the ones described above. Like we said before, people's experiences with bipolar disorder are varied. However, the following stories will help give you a better idea of what a mood episode may look like.

Sue's Story: A Manic Episode

Sue is an accountant. In the middle of tax season she started sleeping less in order to finish paperwork and found that she no longer needed much sleep and still had plenty of energy to work. In fact, she started sleeping only two hours a night and still found that she had so much energy that she was easily distracted from her work. She got extremely annoyed when several of her clients told her she was talking too fast and that they couldn't follow what she was saying, so she decided to abandon her practice and move to a different state in order to find new clients who were less irritating. In the process of the move, she spent her life savings.

Joe's Story: A Depressive Episode

Ever since his father passed away, Joe had found the holidays challenging. From Thanksgiving until New Year's he felt sad and empty, slept all the time, and isolated himself from his friends and family. The dishes piled up in the sink because he didn't have the energy to wash them. He didn't have an appetite and had to force himself to eat. Joe spent most of his time feeling guilty about arguments he had with his father as a child. Throughout his depression, he felt like he had no purpose in life.

TYPES OF BIPOLAR DISORDER

You may have heard treatment providers refer to bipolar disorder with a number—bipolar I or II—or with the word "cyclothymia." This is because there are different types of bipolar disorder. Each is defined by different levels of manic symptoms, and some also include symptoms of depression. We will describe these diagnoses below, but the key differences between the types of bipolar disorder are the severity and duration of symptoms.

Bipolar I

Bipolar I disorder is characterized by at least one manic episode during your lifetime. You need not have a history of depression to be diagnosed with bipolar I disorder. This may seem confusing, since the word "bipolar" implies fluctuating between two moods and the illness is sometimes referred to as manic-depressive disorder. Nonetheless, the only criterion for bipolar I disorder is at least one episode of mania. Although it's not required for the diagnosis, depression is very common in bipolar I. About two-thirds of people with bipolar I disorder experience a depressive episode in their lifetime (Cuellar, Johnson, and Winters 2005), so in bipolar I disorder it is common to experience both depressive and manic episodes.

Bipolar II

Bipolar II disorder is defined by experiencing both a hypomanic and a depressive episode. In other words, to meet the criteria for bipolar II, a previous episode of depression is necessary, along with symptoms of less intense mania lasting at least four days. If a person has experienced both hypomanic and manic episodes, he is diagnosed with bipolar I disorder, not with bipolar II disorder.

Cyclothymia

Cyclothymia is defined by a pattern of chronic and frequent mood changes. These fluctuations are not as extreme as those experienced in manic episodes. Rather, the diagnosis is based on how much of the time some type of changed mood is present. People with cyclothymia tend to feel either up or down at least half of the time. Cyclothymia isn't diagnosed until those mood fluctuations have continued for a long time: one year for adolescents and two years for adults.

THE EXPERIENCE OF BIPOLAR DISORDER OVER TIME

Bipolar disorder is an episodic, recurrent illness. This means that throughout your life, you might experience symptoms of mania or depression, and then these symptoms will clear and you will experience periods of wellness. Often, this pattern tends to repeat itself. *Relapse* refers to a new episode after your first episode of mania or depression. *Remission* or *euthymia* refers to periods without manic or depressive symptoms.

Even if you do everything you can to take care of yourself, you may have relapses. However, they will be less frequent if you take good care of yourself by doing things such as taking your medications, working with your treatment providers, getting enough sleep, and identifying changes in your mood. The goal of treatment is for you to learn how to minimize the chances of having another episode. While there currently is no cure for bipolar disorder, many effective treatments exist (discussed in chapters 3 and 4). Thanks to these treatments, many people who in the past would have spent a lot of time hospitalized can manage their illness and continue living their lives and achieving their goals.

THE BIOLOGY OF BIPOLAR DISORDER

As we stated at the beginning of this chapter, bipolar disorder is a biological illness. Although we know that bipolar disorder results from biological changes, there are currently no medical tests, such as brain scans, blood tests, or genetic tests, that can confirm a bipolar diagnosis or the likelihood of developing the illness. Stressors such as childhood trauma, poor family relationships, and sleep deprivation can bring on or worsen symptoms, but they don't cause bipolar disorder. In this section, we'll discuss the biological changes that are believed to contribute to the development of this illness.

Changes in Brain Chemistry

Bipolar disorder is an illness related to the chemistry of the brain. Research has shown that among those with bipolar disorder, some *neurotransmitters*—the chemicals that carry information throughout the brain and nervous system—don't appear to work properly. Two important neurotransmitters that are disrupted in bipolar disorder are dopamine and serotonin. *Dopamine* is related to the reward system and plays a role in wanting something, such as achieving an important goal. *Serotonin* is related to mood regulation and helps keep you from having too many highs and lows. Problems with the dopamine and serotonin systems are believed to cause changes in mood and behaviors. Medications that help balance mood work by restoring these systems in the brain. (We'll discuss these medications in chapter 3.)

Areas of the brain that regulate mood and the reward system are also affected in bipolar disorder. As a result, it becomes more difficult to modify your mood in response to your situation. It may be easier to think of these parts of your brain as a thermostat for your mood. In your home, the thermostat helps keep the temperature of a room stable by making changes in response to the environment. If your house is hotter than the set temperature, the thermostat will turn on the air-conditioning, and if your house is colder, it will turn on the heat. Your brain's mood thermostat is in charge of keeping your mood stable and appropriate to your situation.

Genes and Bipolar Disorder

Whether people develop bipolar disorder can be highly influenced by their genes. The heritability of this illness is 70 to 80 percent (Gurling et al. 1995), which means that 70 to 80 percent of the risk of developing bipolar disorder is genetic. It also means that about 20 to 30 percent of the risk of developing bipolar disorder is driven by factors other than genes. We know that bipolar disorder involves many genes, but researchers are still trying to identify the particular combinations of genes involved. Therefore, it's difficult to pinpoint the exact cause of developing this illness for a particular person.

Bipolar disorder is thought to result from a combination of genetic vulnerabilities and environmental influences. In some environments a person may not develop symptoms, despite having the genes for bipolar disorder. In other environments, the genes for bipolar disorder may be expressed, showing up in the form of symptoms.

About 1 percent of people have bipolar I disorder, and about 4 percent of people experience other types of bipolar disorder (bipolar II or cyclothymia; Merikangas et al. 2007). Even though the disorder is genetically influenced, most children who have a parent with bipolar disorder will not develop the disorder. Having a parent with bipolar disorder increases the risk for bipolar disorder, on average, fourfold to sixfold (Nurnberger and Foroud 2000). Needless to say, you can't choose whether your child will inherit the disorder, just like you can't choose the color of your child's eyes. However, you can learn strategies to provide a supportive environment if your child does develop the illness. You can also help your child learn as much as possible about how to regulate moods.

Even if you don't have a history of this illness in your family, changes that occur in development before birth can impact your genes and the likelihood that you'll develop an illness like bipolar disorder. In addition, it's possible that family members with experiences similar to yours who may have had bipolar disorder but were never diagnosed.

Genetics and neurotransmitters can be scary topics to learn about; people sometimes feel like this information implies that they have no control over their moods or their lives. Some people also mistakenly believe that because bipolar disorder has a strong genetic component, it cannot be helped. This isn't true. By making it a priority to learn more about your illness and by doing things like reading this book, you are taking charge of your life and learning skills to manage the illness and stay healthy. You're also putting yourself in a position to educate your family members and friends about bipolar disorder.

COMMON CO-OCCURRING DISORDERS AND SYMPTOMS

Sometimes when you have an illness you may also experience other disorders or symptoms. Two or more disorders that occur at the same time are known as *comorbid disorders*. Comorbid disorders that tend to occur with bipolar disorder can make it more difficult to manage your symptoms. However, educating yourself about these additional disorders or symptoms can help you prolong periods of wellness.

Other Mental Illnesses

More than 50 percent of people with bipolar disorder experience severe anxiety (Simon et al. 2004). In addition, 60 percent of people with bipolar disorder have recurrent problems with or become addicted to alcohol or drugs at some point in their lifetime (Regier et al. 1990). People with bipolar disorder may have the most severe problems with anxiety, alcohol, or drugs during mood episodes. When you feel manic, you may be particularly vulnerable to excessive drug or alcohol use because of the tendency to get overly involved in pleasurable activities or sensation seeking. Other problems that tend to co-occur with bipolar disorder are eating disorders (McElroy et al. 2001) and attention deficit/hyperactivity disorder (Nierenberg et al. 2005).

Sometimes people with bipolar disorder report strange or unusual sensations called *psychotic features*. This may sound scary, but it's actually very common. Psychotic features typically involve seeing or hearing something that others cannot (hallucinations) or having beliefs that aren't supported by facts (delusions). Examples of delusions would be thinking that you're fluent in a language that you haven't studied before or believing that you've created an equation that will solve a financial crisis even though you've never studied economics. In bipolar disorder, these psychotic experiences occur during manic or depressive episodes and then clear when the mood symptoms get better.

You can learn more about these comorbid mental disorders by talking to other people who have had such experiences or by taking a class on symptoms, coping strategies, and treatment options. This is often referred to as *psychoeducation*, and we will discuss it further in chapter 4. You may also find some of the books and websites listed in the Resources section helpful.

Other Medical Illnesses

Bipolar disorder is also related to high rates of medical illnesses. Cardiovascular conditions such as heart disease, high blood pressure, and elevated cholesterol occur much more frequently in people with bipolar disorder than in the general population (Kupfer 2005). In addition, there is an increased risk for weight gain, often due to side effects of medications prescribed to treat mood fluctuations. Therefore, it's helpful for people with bipolar disorder to communicate regularly with their doctors to find a balance in their medications that allows for greater benefits (stable mood and fewer mood episodes) and fewer negative side effects, including weight gain. If you experience any of these comorbid medical illnesses or symptoms, discuss them with your treatment team to learn more about how you can manage your physical health.

MYTHS ABOUT BIPOLAR DISORDER

Now that you've learned the basics about what bipolar disorder is, what it looks like, and what we know about its causes, you have the knowledge to dispel some of the common myths about bipolar disorder and educate others about this illness. Let's take a look at some of these myths.

Myth: If I were stronger, I wouldn't have this illness.

Reality: We know that bipolar disorder is a biological illness. It is largely caused by genetics and a chemical imbalance in the parts of the brain that help regulate mood. Bipolar disorder isn't a weakness; it's linked to actual biological changes in your body.

Myth: I'll never be able to reach my goals because I have bipolar disorder.

Reality: Now that more is known about what causes bipolar disorder and helpful treatments have been developed, people with bipolar disorder often live healthy, fulfilling lives and continue to meet their life goals.

Myth: Something I did caused this illness.

Reality: Because bipolar disorder is a biological illness, nothing you did *caused* you to develop symptoms. Although factors like stressful or exciting life events or sleep deprivation may make it more likely that you'll experience symptoms, they don't cause the illness.

Myth: I can control this illness without medications and doctors.

Reality: While you hold the power to manage your illness, taking medications and working with a treatment team will help you cope with symptoms, lengthen your periods of being symptom-free, and decrease the number and severity of future mood episodes. That is why we highly recommend working with mental health professionals if your goal is to recover and stay well.

SUMMARY

Bipolar disorder is a biological illness that affects your ability to regulate your mood. To receive a bipolar disorder diagnosis, a person must experience a combination of manic symptoms for a certain period of time. Many people with bipolar disorder also struggle with depressive symptoms. Since bipolar disorder is a recurrent disorder, episodes of mania or depression tend to repeat over time. Identifying the symptoms that are most common for you and actively engaging in treatment will help to extend periods of wellness between mood episodes. Although there are misconceptions about the causes and symptoms of bipolar disorder, many people with this diagnosis prove these myths wrong by living meaningful and satisfying lives.

CHAPTER 2

RECEIVING A DIAGNOSIS AND FINDING HELP

Receiving a diagnosis of bipolar disorder, or any other illness for that matter, is often challenging and may bring up many different emotions. You may feel scared because bipolar disorder is a life-long illness, or you may feel relieved because you've struggled with symptoms for a long time and now your experiences have a name. A diagnosis is the first step in receiving treatment that will help you take control of your mood and maintain longer periods of wellness. In this chapter, we'll help you prepare to take that first step. We'll provide you with resources to help you find treatment providers and prepare for that first appointment, including questions your clinician may ask. We'll also try to give you an idea of what to expect after receiving a diagnosis or beginning treatment.

FINDING PROFESSIONAL HELP

A variety of helpful resources and professionals are available to provide support for those with bipolar disorder. Some people decide to work with multiple skilled professionals who specialize in various components of their treatment. An example of a treatment team may include a psychiatrist who prescribes medication, a therapist who offers weekly support, and a caseworker who helps coordinate services. An ideal approach is to find treatment providers who already work together, preferably in the same center. This will help ensure that your treatment team works closely together to provide the best care. Often though, the treatment team approach isn't available in a given area, or you may find that you really like one provider who isn't part of a larger team. If members of your treatment team don't work in the same place, it's a good idea to provide written permission for members of your treatment team to talk to each other. This way, they can work collaboratively to provide the best quality of care. The goal is to work with people you feel comfortable with who are also able to help you navigate the variety of available treatment options so you can make informed decisions about your health care. Finding the treatment providers who are right for you can take time, but in a way this is good news because it means you have a lot of options.

Types of Mental Health Professionals

Doctors, psychiatrists, and therapists, oh my! Selecting a treatment provider can be confusing if you don't know the difference between the types of services and help various mental health professionals can offer. When researching possible treatment providers, pay special attention to their degrees, training, and specialties. This information will help determine the kind of help they can offer and what types of treatment services they provide.

MEDICATION PROVIDERS

Psychiatrists, who hold medical degrees such as MD, are treatment providers who can prescribe medications, much like your primary care physician. However, they also have specialized training in diagnosing and treating mental illness. Since most people with bipolar disorder decide to take medication to help treat their symptoms and extend periods of wellness, it's likely that you'll have a psychiatrist on your treatment team. Typically, you'll see your psychiatrist about once a month or less for medication checkups, or sooner if you have a medication emergency. Alternatively, you may choose to receive medication advice and prescriptions from your primary care physician. Although this is often a more convenient and affordable way to get medications, these doctors don't have the specialized training in mental illness that psychiatrists receive as part of their medical training.

THERAPY AND SUPPORT

As we'll discuss in chapter 4, there are a variety of different types of therapy, and several that are especially effective for bipolar disorder. *Therapist* is a term used to describe anyone who provides talk therapy (for example, a psychologist or social worker). Just as there are different therapy styles, therapists have different training backgrounds and experience. You'll have to do some research to find therapists in your area who are skilled and knowledgeable about bipolar disorder; however, we have provided some information to help you in your search, both in this chapter and in the Resources section.

Psychologists, who hold degrees such as PhD or PsyD, are doctors who have received extensive training in mental illness, just like psychiatrists, but their specialty is in therapy, not medication. In some states (currently just New Mexico and Louisiana), psychologists can receive additional training that allows them to prescribe medications. Check with local psychologists to see if you can receive therapy and medication services from one provider.

Social workers, marriage and family therapists, and *caseworkers*, who hold degrees such as MSW, MFT, or LCSW, also receive specialized training in working with people with mental illness diagnoses. They can offer therapy and support and can also help with navigating government and community services.

Nurse practitioners, who hold degrees such as NP-C, ARNP, CNP, and PMHNP, can also offer psychological services and often work closely with psychiatrists to coordinate care. They receive additional training in diagnosing and treating both medical and mental illnesses and can also prescribe medications. Although it is important to know that they have less specialized training in medications than psychiatrists, many nurse practitioners are more available at short notice in times of crisis.

Getting Referrals and Recommendations

Finding a mental health professional can be relatively easy if you know where to look. If you have insurance, you may want to start by researching the services and treatment providers covered by your insurance plan. You can also learn about services in your area through organizations you trust. The Depression and Bipolar Support Alliance (DBSA) has created a Find a Pro search engine; it can help you find treatment providers in your area who have been recommended by other people with bipolar disorder (find-apro.dbsapages.org). The National Network of Depression Centers website is another resource that can help you find organizations in your area that specialize in the treatment of depression (www.nndc.org/centers-of-excellence). University hospitals and Veterans Affairs medical centers often have specialized clinics that can offer care to individuals with bipolar disorder. Finally, resources for finding therapists in your area are also available on the websites of professional psychological organizations, such as the American Psychological Association (locator.apa.org) and the Association for Behavioral and Cognitive Therapies (abct.org).

CHOOSING A BIPOLAR DISORDER SPECIALIST

There's a lot to think about before making that first call to sched-ule an appointment with a mental health professional. Take some time and research all of your options before making a decision about whom you'd like to have on your team. The choice to get help and whom you work with is yours, so set yourself up for suc-cess by finding treatment providers who support and understand you. If you are restricted in your treatment options because of your insurance plan, finances, or availability of resources, it is still important to research the providers who are available to you. Learning more about the kind of treatment team you want may help you feel more comfortable, prepared, and in control when you show up for the first appointment.

Also remember that you have options. When beginning your search, it's a good idea to meet with a couple of different providers before selecting a psychiatrist or therapist. Meeting them in per-son will give you a better idea of who would be a good choice for you. We recommend working with a treatment team that can offer both medication and therapy services. As you'll discover as you read further, a combination of medication and psychosocial treatments is often the most effective way to prevent future mood episodes and extend periods of wellness.

INVOLVING YOUR INSURANCE COMPANY

If you have insurance, you'll also need to decide whether you want the insurance company to help pay for services. However, some insurance companies limit the number of visits they'll cover, so if you're looking for long-term care, you may not want to start treatment with someone who will be able to provide treatment for only as long as your insurance company allows.

The services that are paid for by your insurance company will also be on record, which means that, just as with any other illness, anyone who is associated with the treatment center or insurance company could potentially have access to these files, your diagnosis, and the treatment you received. It is important to always read the privacy notices you receive when you begin treatment with a new provider or at a new health center. These describe how your information is stored and who can access it. If you pay for services yourself, you have more freedom about where you receive treatment, and possibly more privacy regarding your treatment history. Unfortunately, private mental health services tend to be more expensive, so your choices and treatment might be restricted by which services you can afford.

SCHEDULING AN APPOINTMENT

After selecting the treatment providers you'd like to consult with, the next step is scheduling an appointment. Whomever you talk to when scheduling the appointment will probably ask you some brief questions about the services you're looking for and why you're currently looking for support; for example, "When did you first notice there was a problem?" and "What have you done in the past to help deal with these experiences?" These questions will vary depending upon whom you call. If you're contacting someone from a large medical group, such as Kaiser Permanente, this phone call may be short. If you're contacting someone at a small center or community clinic or an individual, such as a mental health professional in private practice, the person who takes your call may collect more information to determine whether they can provide the services you're looking for before scheduling an appointment.

It may take some time to schedule an appointment if you have to leave messages or play phone tag before getting someone on the phone. Then, when you do make contact, you may not be able to schedule an appointment right away depending on availability or finding a time that works with your schedule. This can be frustrating. If this occurs, try to generate creative solutions and adjust your schedule as needed to take advantage of an available appointment time. You may need to take a day off of work, arrange for child care, or otherwise free up time in your schedule.

You may also find that there are no openings with a particular doctor or center. If this is the case, they will probably give you referrals to other agencies and treatment providers in the area. They may also offer to place you on a waiting list and contact you when they have availability. Although this is less than ideal, it's probably worth doing. While you wait, you can continue to contact other treatment providers, using their referrals as a starting point. Since scheduling an appointment may take some time, it is helpful to contact multiple treatment providers whom you may be interested in working with.

PREPARING FOR THE APPOINTMENT

The goal of the initial consultation with a bipolar disorder specialist is for the care provider to learn more about your history and experiences. This first session with a doctor or therapist is often the longest. For example, you may need to arrive early to read and complete paperwork, such as consent forms and the privacy policies we mentioned earlier. The provider will ask you questions about your symptoms, the history of your concerns, and any family history of mental illness. If you've struggled with mood symptoms for a long time, you will probably need more than one session to cover all of this material with a new treatment provider. Taking time to think about your history before your appointment will help move the process along.

The first appointment is also a time for you to ask questions about the services that will be provided and any concerns you may have regarding your treatment or health. To prepare for the appointment, it would be a good idea to read chapters 3 and 4 of this book so you are more informed about your medication and treatment options.

Information You May Want to Bring

To help prepare for this first appointment, spend some time thinking about your experiences with each of the symptoms discussed in chapter 1, both currently and throughout your life. Did any of the symptoms we talked about stand out to you? Have your moods, behaviors, or thoughts ever caused you problems or made it more difficult for you to get through the day? The mental health professional you meet with will want to hear about these challenges, so write them down or start a list you can bring with you to this first session. You can also talk to family members about concerns they may have or things they've noticed that would be helpful for you to talk about with your treatment provider. If this isn't your first time receiving mental health services, you'll also discuss your previous treatments so your provider can learn more about which medications and treatments have helped in the past. If you have taken medications for mental health issues in the past, bring a list of those medications with you. If possible, provide a list of what dosages you took of each medication, how much relief you noticed, and whether you experienced any side effects. The more you can share about previous treatments, the better.

Bringing a Support Person

Meeting a treatment provider for the first time can be stressful, so you may want to bring someone along for support. If there's someone who you feel understands you, who has been there for you while you struggled with mood symptoms, or who offered help along the way, you may want to bring this person with you to the appointment. It's fine to ask mental health professionals if they would like you to bring another person to join the initial consultation. In fact, it is often helpful for treatment providers to hear another person's perspective.

Providers may also ask to talk to family members or significant others later in treatment if you agree that it might help your treatment. If bringing someone to the actual session isn't an option, you can always bring someone along for support before and afterward. Since waiting rooms are often small, we recommend bringing only one person with you.

DURING THE APPOINTMENT

As mentioned earlier, the first time you meet with a treatment provider you'll have to answer important questions about your background and experiences. The information you provide in this session will help your treatment provider learn more about you and determine whether what you describe is consistent with a diagnosis of bipolar disorder. Don't be dismayed if it feels like the initial session doesn't help. It can sometimes take several sessions for a mental health professional to conduct a comprehensive diagnostic interview and carefully collect all the information necessary to make a diagnosis and design a good treatment plan. Although it may not feel like it, the time it takes for care providers to learn about your experiences is an essential component not only of your diagnosis but also of treatment.

Testing and Assessments

As mentioned, there are no medical tests (such as brain scans or blood tests) that can confirm a diagnosis of bipolar disorder. Instead, treatment providers will ask you lots of questions about your experiences and the length of time you've had symptoms to determine whether the frequency, severity, and timing of your mood symptoms meet the diagnostic criteria for bipolar disorder. You may also be referred to a physician for a physical exam and thorough medical history in order to rule out other illnesses that might be causing your symptoms; for example, thyroid problems can cause mood swings.

Questions You May Be Asked

To help you prepare for your appointment, we'll list some of the questions that mental health professionals will ask to learn more about your mood, symptoms of mania and depression, and other symptoms or concerns. While some of these questions may seem invasive or embarrassing, it's important to answer openly and honestly so the care provider has an accurate picture of your experiences and can offer you the most effective treatments. Think about how you would answer these questions given your past and current experiences:

- Has there been a period of time when you felt down or depressed? How long did that last? Tell me more about that experience.

- How about the opposite: Have you ever felt so good, high, or excited that others thought you weren't your usual self or felt concerned about you? Describe what else was going on during that time.

- When you were feeling unusually sad or elated, did you notice any changes in your sleep? What about your appetite?

- Have there been times when you felt unusually irritable—more than just waking up on the wrong side of the bed? Did you find yourself starting arguments with your friends or family members? How about strangers?

- When you were feeling irritable or unusually high, did you or others notice any changes in the way you talked? For example, did you talk louder or faster? Was it hard for others to get a word in? Did you feel like your thoughts were changing so fast that it was hard for you to communicate what you were thinking?

- What was your energy like? Did you lie in bed a lot or feel slower than usual? What about the opposite: Did you have lots of energy? Did you start a lot of projects? Did you have a lot of goals you were working toward?

- How was your self-esteem during these times? Did you think you were better, worse, or about the same as others?

- Have you felt nervous or anxious lately?

- How often do you consume alcohol? How much? How often do you use nonprescribed drugs, such as marijuana, cocaine, or heroin? How does using drugs or alcohol affect your mood or symptoms?

- Do you have any other concerns?

Family History

As discussed in chapter 1, genes can influence your likelihood of developing bipolar disorder. Learning more about your family history of mental illness, particularly any history of bipolar disorder or depression, will provide your treatment team with very helpful diagnostic information. You may not know of any family members who received an official diagnosis, but your clinician can still gather useful information by asking questions such as "Do you know of anyone in your family who experiences similar problems with mood? Are there family members you've worried about because you haven't heard from them for a while, or who seem different from the rest of the family in some way?" Questions like these will help you and your treatment provider consider whether other people in your family have struggled with their mood, even if they didn't necessarily have a mental illness diagnosis.

Questions You Might Want to Ask

The first appointment with a mental health professional is also an opportunity for you to ask questions and receive answers. Check in with yourself and make sure you feel comfortable working with this treatment provider. Feeling like you click and that you can confide in this person is often a good indicator that you've found a good match. However, it may take more than one session to determine this.

In your initial meetings, be sure to save some time to address any questions or concerns that come up during your time together. Here are some questions you may want to ask:

- What is your experience with treating bipolar disorder?

- What treatment do you recommend? How well do you think it will work?

- What other treatment options are available?

- How often will we meet? How long will our appointments last?

- How can I reach you in case of an emergency?

- What should I do if I forget to take my medication or miss an appointment?

- Is there a generic form of my medication?

AFTER YOUR DIAGNOSIS

Getting a diagnosis of bipolar disorder is the first step toward receiving treatments that can offer relief from symptoms and getting support for staying well. The goal of a diagnostic interview is to help you put together the pieces of your symptoms in a way that helps you understand your previous experiences in a new light. A diagnosis can set you on a path that can help you lead a generally happy and healthy life.

The Good and Bad Aspects of Receiving a Diagnosis

Learning that you have bipolar disorder can be challenging. You may have a lot of questions or fears about the illness. Talking to your treatment team about your concerns and worries can help make this difficult time easier. Unfortunately, there are still a lot of myths and misconceptions about mental illness, often perpetuated by the media and possibly believed by people you know. Sometimes people with bipolar disorder are portrayed as unpredictable, violent, or unable to succeed in life. The good news is that there is a lot of research showing that treatments such as medications and therapy are helpful for people with bipolar disorder and that these myths are false.

Although it may be hard to see at first, a lot of good can come from a bipolar diagnosis. Once you learn skills for managing your mood, your symptoms won't feel as overwhelming, and you may be less likely to engage in activities that have caused you problems before, such as overspending or engaging in risky sexual behavior. People with bipolar disorder can be just as successful as people without mental illness, and staying healthy maximizes the chances of this being the case for you. People with bipolar disorder are also often very creative. Being able to think outside the box can help you come up with a lot of different solutions to problems—including those in your own life. Most importantly, the good aspects of bipolar disorder don't go away with treatment. Treatment simply helps you to manage your illness so you can continue to build a good life for yourself. We'll discuss positive traits associated with bipolar disorder in chapter 8.

The Next Steps

After your initial meeting with a mental health professional, the next step is to think about whether you want to continue to meet with this person and receive regular treatment. The decision is yours, so if you don't feel heard, comfortable, or supported, you may want to continue your search. If you have concerns, you may also want to bring them up with the care provider before deciding to work with someone else. However, if you don't feel like you can talk openly with the treatment provider, that may be a sign that this isn't the best treatment relationship for you. If at any time you decide that you aren't satisfied with your treatment provider or that this person cannot offer the quality of care you're looking for, don't feel guilty about exploring other options, even if you've already started treatment with that provider. A good place to start is by raising your worries, to see if you can improve your relationship with the provider. Your right to receive excellent care is more important than protecting the feelings of mental health care providers. Once you decide on a treatment provider or team, you can begin to learn more about the treatments that are available and start working collaboratively to decide which treatments might be most helpful for you.

SUMMARY

Finding a treatment provider can take time and feel overwhelming, but it's an important first step in receiving a diagnosis and getting professional support. There are many options and resources available to you, so take some time to really research the professionals in your area and find one, or a team, that feels right to you. To prepare for the first session with a mental health professional, it's helpful to think back on your experiences throughout life and the symptoms discussed in chapter 1. Share this information in your initial appointments to help treatment providers learn more about your experiences and determine whether you meet the diagnostic criteria for bipolar disorder. Working with your treatment team can help you manage the concerns you might have after receiving a bipolar disorder diagnosis. Although it's natural to have some fears, a diagnosis can also help you understand your past experiences. It can also be a source of hope, as you can now receive treatments that have been shown to help manage the ups and downs of mood that constitute bipolar disorder.

CHAPTER 3

MEDICATIONS

Medication is the most effective treatment for managing symptoms of bipolar disorder and extending periods of wellness (American Psychiatric Association 2002). When you have fewer mood episodes, you can more effectively work toward your goals, strengthen your relationships with friends and family members, and feel balanced and in control. In addition to medication, psychosocial treatments (discussed in chapter 4) can also help reduce symptoms and improve quality of life. In this chapter, we'll discuss the benefits and side effects of medications approved for treating bipolar disorder and answer some common questions people have about taking medications.

In bipolar disorder, medications are used to relieve acute symptoms of mania or depression. Since mood episodes tend to reoccur, it's often important to take medications even when you aren't manic or depressed. This is called *maintenance treatment*. Learning more about medications will help you become an educated consumer so that you can actively participate with your treatment team in fine-tuning this aspect of your treatment.

THE PROS AND CONS OF TAKING MEDICATIONS

It's completely normal to have concerns about long-term medication treatment. As with any illness and treatment, it's important to educate yourself on the pros and cons of taking medications to treat bipolar disorder. The goal of a good medication plan is to maximize benefits (symptom relief) and minimize costs (side effects). Although medications may help you experience fewer symptoms and mood episodes, they may also cause some unwanted side effects, such as weight gain and fatigue, and they may require certain dietary restrictions. As a consumer, it's your job to weigh the costs and benefits and work with your doctor to find the type of medication and dosage that works best for you. Unfortunately, this often takes time and some trial and error. You may have to try a variety of medications before you find the right one.

Even with all of the benefits of medication, many people struggle with whether to take them and whether to stay on them for long periods. Some medications are expensive; however, most drug companies have programs for receiving medications at a lower cost. Another issue is that sometimes it takes several weeks before you feel the benefits of a medication, and you may actually experience side effects that make you feel worse before you start feeling better.

Most importantly, realize that there's no guarantee that medication will relieve all of your symptoms. Even if you take your medications regularly, there is a chance that you may relapse or experience ongoing mild symptoms. These are all important possibilities to consider when deciding whether to take medications, and there's a good chance that you can think of additional items to add to that list. The good news is, there are coping strategies that will help make the downsides of medication more manageable, and we'll describe some of them below.

FDA-APPROVED MEDICATIONS FOR BIPOLAR DISORDER

Medications for bipolar disorder work by increasing the function of neurotransmitters, the chemicals in the brain that help regulate mood (discussed in chapter 1). In this section we'll discuss medications approved by the Food and Drug Administration (FDA). The FDA is the U.S. federal agency responsible for ensuring that medications provide benefits and are safe for use by the general public. To be approved by the FDA, a drug must go through several stages of review, including tests comparing the drug to a placebo (a sugar pill) to make sure there's evidence that it works better than not taking medication.

Unfortunately, people sometimes advertise or push treatments with no scientific support or FDA approval. For example, you may see advertisements for natural or herbal remedies as substitutions for medications prescribed for bipolar disorder. If you use treatment strategies that haven't been tested, you run a higher risk of having future mood episodes. Using only treatments that have been approved by the FDA will ensure that you're taking medications that researchers have carefully studied and that are known to be effective in preventing symptoms and relapse.

The medications currently available for bipolar disorder aren't perfect. The good news is, there's hope on the horizon. Scientists are constantly working to develop new medications that will be more effective at decreasing symptoms with fewer side effects. We have every expectation that this will bring more relief in the future. To keep yourself updated on newly approved medications, or if you have questions about a medication that this book doesn't address, visit the FDA website (www.fda.gov) or talk to your treatment providers.

Mood Stabilizing Medications

Mood stabilizers are medications that reduce symptoms of mania and depression and help keep your mood balanced between episodes. Lithium carbonate, often referred to as lithium, is the most commonly used mood stabilizer. Lithium works best for people who have had a manic episode (bipolar I disorder; American Psychiatric Association 2002). It's helpful for reducing acute manic symptoms and as a maintenance treatment during periods of wellness. When people are taking lithium, they are also less likely to attempt suicide. In other words, it saves lives. Some people experience side effects from lithium that can include tremors, nausea, weight gain, fatigue, dehydration, dry mouth, diarrhea, and low levels of thyroid hormones. When taking lithium, you'll have to moderate your salt intake so you don't become dehydrated.

As with all medications, it's important to find the dose that works for you. This is particularly important with lithium because if you take too little, it's ineffective, and if you take too much, you can develop lithium toxicity. Symptoms of lithium toxicity include fatigue, slurred speech, and severe tremors. To avoid this, routine blood tests are used to monitor the level of lithium in your blood.

Antiseizure Medications

Antiseizure medications, or *anticonvulsants*, are an alternative type of mood stabilizer often used to treat bipolar disorder. Sometimes they're used when people experience too many side effects from lithium. Carbamazepine (brand name Tegretol), valproic acid (brand name Depakote), topiramate (brand name Topamax), and lamotrigine (brand name Lamictal) are some commonly prescribed antiseizure medications. General side effects can include sedation, nausea, and upset stomach. Topiramate is often prescribed in combination with other mood stabilizers to help offset the side effect of weight gain, but it is associated with more attention, concentration, and memory impairments than other drugs used to treat bipolar disorder (Chengappa et al. 2001). Lamotrigine is most effective for treating depressive episodes in bipolar disorder, helps improve cognitive functioning (Khan et al.

2004), and is often prescribed to pregnant women who have bipolar disorder (Ornoy 2006). Side effects of lamotrigine can include dizziness, tremors, headache, nausea, and rashes.

Antipsychotic Medications

As discussed in chapter 1, psychotic features (hallucinations or delusions) can be a common experience for people in acute manic or depressive episodes. *Antipsychotic medications*, which are also called *neuroleptic medications*, are helpful in reducing psychotic symptoms and lowering irritability, and they can be the fastest way to treat acute manic episodes (American Psychiatric Association 2002). Doctors often prescribe antipsychotic medications when people with bipolar disorder are hospitalized, and some people may continue to use these medications as a maintenance treatment.

There are two main categories of antipsychotic medications, and they differ by when they were created and how they interact with the brain. Chlorpromazine (brand name Thorazine) and haloperidol (brand name Haldol) are commonly referred to as *first-generation antipsychotic medications*. These medications are just as effective at treating symptoms as newer, *second-generation antipsychotics*. They are often cheaper, but they can have some troubling side effects, including dry mouth, sedation, constipation, rigidity, restlessness, and, if used long-term, *tardive dyskinesia*, an irreversible condition that involves abnormal mouth movements.

In an effort to decrease the negative side effects of first-generation antipsychotic medications, scientists developed the second-generation antipsychotic medications, which include risperidone (brand name Risperdal), olanzapine (brand name Zyprexa), quetiapine (brand name Seroquel), and aripiprazole (brand name Abilify). These medications are more commonly used to treat bipolar disorder than first-generation antipsychotic medications but also tend to be more expensive. Side effects associated with second-generation antipsychotic medications include weight gain and, unfortunately, some of the same side effects as the first-generation medications, such as rigidity, restlessness, and sedation.

Antidepressant Medications

It was once thought that *antidepressants* (medications commonly prescribed to treat depressive disorders and anxiety) were necessary to treat bipolar depression. Research now shows that mood stabilizers alone can help with both mania and depression, so taking an antidepressant might not be necessary (Sachs, Sylvia, and Kund 2009; Altshuler et al. 2009). For many people with bipolar disorder, taking an antidepressant without a mood stabilizer can cause a manic episode (Ghaemi, Lenox, and Baldessarini 2001). This risk is lower if antidepressants are taken in combination with other mood stabilizing medications (Sachs et al. 2007). That said, if your mood is stable, don't be alarmed if you're taking antidepressants without a mood stabilizer. This means that the antidepressant you're taking seems to be working, so it isn't necessary to switch medications. Since finding the right medication takes time, it's best not to change a medication if it is working for you. If you do have concerns, be sure to discuss them with your treatment team.

There are several classes of antidepressants. *Selective serotonin reuptake inhibitors* (SSRIs) regulate the serotonin system in the brain. As you probably recall from chapter 1, serotonin is a neurotransmitter involved in mood regulation. Common SSRIs include paroxetine (brand name Paxil), fluoxetine (brand name Prozac), and sertraline (brand name Zoloft). Their side effects can include sexual dysfunction and digestive discomfort. SSRIs are also helpful for treating symptoms of anxiety, which is commonly experienced by individuals with bipolar disorder.

Tricyclic antidepressants, another type of antidepressants, have been used to treat depression for over forty years. Tricyclic antidepressants include imipramine (brand name Tofranil) and clomipramine (brand name Anafranil). Their side effects can include sedation, hypotension, dry mouth, and weight gain.

A third group of antidepressants, classified as *monoamine oxidase inhibitors* (MAOIs), include isocarboxazid (brand name Marplan) and phenelzine (brand name Nardil). MAOIs require a special diet because the chemicals they contain interact with fermented foods and beverages (for example, wine, beer, pickles, fermented cheeses, and cured meats), so doctors typically choose to prescribe other medications.

Lastly, bupropion (brand name Wellbutrin), venlafaxine (brand name Effexor), and duloxetine (brand name Cymbalta) are just as effective as other antidepressants at treating symptoms of depression but are classified separately because they affect different chemicals in the brain. Side effects of these medications can include headaches, nausea, sleep problems, agitation, and sexual dysfunction.

RISKS WITH STOPPING MEDICATIONS

Thinking about stopping the use of medications, or even actually stopping, is very common. It's something most people go through even when taking nonpsychiatric drugs, such as medication for high blood pressure. Research has shown that seven out of every ten people with bipolar disorder stop taking their medication at some point, and nine out of every ten seriously consider discontinuing medication treatment (Colom and Vieta 2006). Unfortunately, stopping medication often results in another mood episode, usually within the next six months to one year, and also increases the risk of suicide attempts (Tondo and Baldessarini 2000).

Stopping medications too quickly and without the guidance of a doctor can also make you feel physically or emotionally sick. If you abruptly stop taking SSRIs (antidepressants such as fluoxetine and sertraline), you may experience flu-like symptoms, sleep disturbances, or digestive discomfort. This is called *serotonin withdrawal syndrome*. This doesn't occur because you've become addicted to the medication; you can't become addicted to antidepressants. Rather, this occurs because you suddenly stopped taking the medication, which affects the serotonin system in your brain. Missing one day is unlikely to trigger this response, so don't panic if this happens.

If you want to stop taking your medication or are experiencing troublesome side effects, talk with your doctor about other options, such as gradually stopping a medication or switching to a new one.

ELECTROCONVULSIVE THERAPY

For some individuals, medications and therapy may be less helpful for treating their symptoms of bipolar disorder. In such cases, doctors sometimes prescribe *electroconvulsive therapy* (ECT), a medical treatment that involves sending a low-level electric current through the brain for about one minute to induce a small seizure. This is commonly conducted in a hospital under the care of physicians. ECT is usually tried when other treatments don't work, and it can be especially helpful for those experiencing severe depression. Researchers don't fully understand why this treatment works, but it seems to help balance mood and decrease mood symptoms. It is also used to treat acute mania and usually results in rapid improvements without the side effects associated with taking mood stabilizing medications. However, short-term memory loss may occur, which usually lasts only a few short weeks after treatment. If you are interested in learning more about the benefits and side effects of ECT, talk to your treatment provider.

QUESTIONS ABOUT MEDICATIONS

It's likely that you still have questions or concerns about taking medication. Having questions is a good thing; it means you're actively participating in decisions about your treatment. We'll answer some of the most common questions people have about medications below. Since we probably won't answer all of your questions, we recommend that you work with your treatment team to address any additional concerns you may have.

Question: Are bipolar medications addictive?

Answer: Addiction is a common concern. However, there is no risk of developing an addiction to the medications that doctors prescribe to help balance mood, such as mood stabilizers, antiseizure medications, antipsychotic medications, and antidepressants. These medications alter the chemicals in your brain in a different way than addictive drugs, such as nicotine, alcohol, or some nonprescribed drugs do. Some prescription medications, such as particular antianxiety and sleep medications, do have the potential to become addictive. However, doctors are trained to prescribe these medications with caution. If you're worried about developing an addiction to a particular medication, you should discuss your concerns with your doctor.

Question: How do I talk with my psychiatrist about changing my medications?

Answer: As mentioned in chapter 2, it's best to work with a doctor you feel comfortable talking to about your concerns. It's up to you to advocate for yourself and make sure your concerns are heard. Although your doctor is the expert regarding medications and health issues, you're the expert on your experiences. If you feel the side effects of a medication are too much to handle, if you don't like the way a medication makes you feel, or if you want to stop taking medication altogether, your doctor's role is to help you make safe and informed changes to your treatment plan. This can happen only if you speak up and express your concerns. Discuss any worries you may have, such as concerns about risks associated with taking a medication for an extended period or during pregnancy. And if you have upcoming vacations or plans to move to a new city or state, be sure to consult with your doctor about how to make sure you continue to take medications consistently during the transition.

Question: How can I be sure my medications are working?

Answer: We recommend tracking your mood, energy, and side effects (this tracking is discussed in chapter 5) to gain a more objective assessment of how well your treatment program is working. This will help you and your doctor notice changes in your symptoms and document any unwanted side effects.

Question: If I'm feeling better, do I have to keep taking medications?

Answer: It is human nature to think, *I feel better, so I must be better*. However, medications are the best weapon against future mood episodes. For medications to work and prevent relapse, you should take them on a daily basis so there will be a consistent level of medication in your system. This is what helps keep you from experiencing symptoms. If you stop your medications when you feel better and start taking them when symptoms return, it may be too late to prevent a depressive or manic episode, as it can take a couple weeks for the medications to start working again. Research has shown that people who don't take their medications regularly are three times more likely to be hospitalized for a future mood episode (Scott 2002).

Question: How can I remember to take my medications?

Answer: Remembering to take medications every day is a challenge for most people. The good news is, there are several things you can do to make it easier. For example, some medications are available in a time-release or extended-release form (Seroquel XR, Depakote ER). They are released slowly, throughout the day, so you don't have to remember to take pills as often. You can also set up reminders on your phone or computer. Another option is to create a routine to help you remember when to take your medications. For example, you could try taking your medications each evening when you brush your teeth, or you could leave the pills on your nightstand so you can take them as soon as you wake up. If you take your medication at lunchtime, you can keep some pills at your office so you don't have to remember to take them with you to work each day. You can also organize weekly pillboxes at the beginning of each week or two so that you can easily tell if you took your medications on a given day.

Question: How can I deal with side effects?

Answer: Side effects are most extreme during the first two weeks of taking a medication, and many of them tend to go away as your body gets used to the medication. If side effects continue, your doctor may change the medication or prescribe additional medications to help treat the side effects. For example, you may take a different medication to treat weight gain, which is a common side effect of mood stabilizing medications. Although it is impossible to eliminate all of the side effects you may experience, you can do various things to help make them more bearable. For instance, adding exercise to your routine or improving your diet can help with weight gain or feelings of fatigue. You can eat sugar-free hard candy to decrease the discomfort of dry mouth. Some people feel embarrassed by hand tremors that can be a side effect of some medications; if that's the case for you, you could use credit cards rather than checks or money when in public so that people aren't as likely to see your unsteady hands. For side effects of sedation and fatigue, you can take medications at night. If you feel like you can't tolerate a side effect, talk with your doctor to see if there are other options available before discontinuing the medication.

SUMMARY

There are many different types of medications used to treat bipolar disorder. The bad news is that this can be confusing initially. The good news is that there are many different options, so if one medication doesn't work for you, there are others you can try. We hope this chapter has given you the knowledge and resources to become actively involved in decisions about medication and the confidence to start an honest dialogue with your doctor if you have any concerns about the medications prescribed for you.

CHAPTER 4

PSYCHOSOCIAL TREATMENTS THAT WORK

As discussed in chapter 3, research shows that medication is the most well-supported and effective treatment for bipolar mania and depression. However, medication is often only one part of the overall treatment for bipolar disorder. And just as it's very helpful to know about current recommendations on medications, it's also important to be informed about other treatments, how they work, and how helpful they are for treating symptoms.

In this chapter, we'll discuss other treatments that, *when combined with medication*, have been shown to increase the chances of preventing future mood episodes and prolonging periods of well-ness. These are commonly referred to as *psychosocial treatments* because they involve a combination of psychological and social interventions. You'll also hear them referred to as *talk therapies* or *psychotherapies.* Remember, different treatments and combinations of treatments are more effective for different individuals. While we can't recommend which form of psychotherapy will work best for you, we can explain what's involved with each so you can work with your treatment team to make an informed decision about what treatment might be most helpful for you.

PROVEN PSYCHOSOCIAL TREATMENTS

Research supports the effectiveness of several psychosocial treatments for bipolar disorder, including psychoeducation, cognitive behavioral therapy, family-focused therapy, and interpersonal and social rhythm therapy. All four of these treatments have been found to decrease symptoms of depression, while psychoeducation seems to be equally effective for decreasing both mania and depression symptoms. All four treatments decrease the chances of hospitalization, and all of them also help people rebuild their social world after a manic episode. However, it is important to remember that medication is still the best and quickest treatment for reducing symptoms of mania and preventing their return. Talk therapies can be used as a supplement to medication.

Psychoeducation

Psychoeducation involves increasing your knowledge about bipolar disorder, its causes, and how clinicians diagnose and treat it. You learn about the features of bipolar disorder, how to recognize symptoms, how to identify triggers of mania and depression, and how to minimize the chances of experiencing another mood episode. Psychoeducation includes helping you develop strategies to ensure you take your medication and engage in behaviors that help you stay healthy, such as getting enough sleep and identifying early warning signs of an oncoming mood episode. It also teaches you to minimize the experiences that put you at risk for relapse (for example, by reducing stress and substance use and using effective problem-solving strategies when necessary) and helps you plan for what to do if you do become depressed or manic. You may be thinking that many of these topics are included in this book, and you're right—reading this book is a component of psychoeducation!

There are three types of psychoeducation: individual, group, and family, all of which involve working with a therapist. The first two are designed to provide psychoeducation to those with bipolar disorder. Individual psychoeducation can be incorporated into one-on-one therapy between you and your therapist. Group psychoeducation involves learning about bipolar disorder together with other people who also have the illness. The group approach can provide you with additional support from people who understand what it feels like to have similar experiences and can also help decrease any stigma you might feel about having a diagnosis of bipolar disorder.

When combined with medication, psychoeducation can help decrease your chances of having a future episode of mania or depression, reduce the amount of time you spend in manic or hypomanic episodes, and make it less likely that you'll be hospitalized (Colom and Vieta 2006). Psychoeducation is a component of all of the other psychosocial interventions we discuss in this chapter.

The third type of psychoeducation is for family members of people with bipolar disorder. Family psychoeducation may be offered to family members individually or to a group of family members. Either way, your family members can work with a mental health professional to learn about the disorder and how to support you in staying well.

Cognitive Behavioral Therapy

Individual therapy can help you stay well and provide support as you learn more about your diagnosis and your particular symptoms. Cognitive behavioral therapy (CBT) is the most carefully studied form of individual therapy for depression and is also effective for treating both depression and mania in bipolar disorder. CBT is a type of talk therapy that focuses on patterns of thoughts, feelings, and behaviors and helping people identify the relationship between those patterns and the symptoms they experience (Beck 1964).

When you're depressed, CBT helps you identify the negative thinking that may be contributing to your mood and helps you work on changing your thoughts and behaviors to improve your mood. Let's walk through an example of what CBT looks like. Let's say that when you're depressed you have little motivation to go to work. You think to yourself, *If I wasn't so awful, I'd be able to do my job like everyone else*. This thought leads you to feel sad, hopeless, and generally bad about yourself (feelings), so you call in sick and isolate yourself from other people (behaviors). These thoughts, feelings, and behaviors reinforce each other. For example, staying home (behavior) reinforces your thought that you don't do your job well, and spending so much time alone (another behavior) makes you feel lonely, so you end up feeling worse.

Cognitive Behavioral Therapy Model (adapted from Beck 1964)

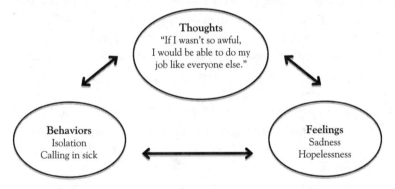

Continuing with this example, in CBT, you would work with your therapist to recognize your tendency to think in negative ways and identify how your thoughts lead to feeling unproductive and helpless. Your therapist would help you identify and change these negative thoughts and set goals to get work done and increase the amount of time you spend with others. Together, these strategies could start to improve your mood and decrease your negative thoughts and feelings.

Depending on your symptoms and goals, CBT can also include coming up with strategies to target the overly positive thinking that's common in mania. CBT may help you learn behavioral strategies to decrease the risk of mania, such as reducing social stimulation and exciting activities when your mood begins to feel high. Other facets of CBT involve learning practical skills to protect yourself from making risky financial or interpersonal decisions once your mood is high—for example, placing a limit on your credit cards or even making them unavailable for a couple of days. Some people we know actually freeze their credit cards in a tray of water; by the time the cards have thawed out of the ice, the urge to spend has usually passed. You may also learn to minimize other consequences of feeling manic—for example, by avoiding large crowds or interactions with new people on days when your mood is high. While these kinds of strategies are important for assisting you in understanding and changing manic behaviors to stay healthy and minimize negative impacts of manic episodes, CBT is most helpful for reducing the frequency and duration of depressive episodes.

There is also some evidence that CBT is most beneficial for people in the early stages of bipolar disorder. This is one reason it's helpful to educate yourself on treatment options as early as possible (Scott 2001). Additionally, sometimes people use CBT to address other types of difficulties beyond depression and mania, such as managing anxiety, and this is an option you can discuss with your treatment team.

Family-Focused Therapy

Family-focused therapy (FFT) is a type of treatment that combines psychoeducation with family therapy. In FFT, individuals with bipolar disorder and their families work together to learn about the features of bipolar disorder, how to recognize and decrease symptoms, and healthy ways to support the person with the diagnosis. FFT also focuses on how family relationships, conflicts, and the emotions family members express to each other can either help or hinder the well-being of the person with bipolar disorder. In these ways, FFT helps families maximize strategies for staying well.

Family-Focused Therapy Model

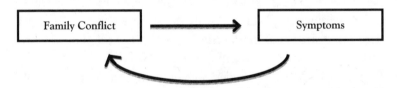

For example, in FFT you and your family might work together to improve your communication styles by practicing and improving skills for listening, expressing feelings, and requesting behavior change. FFT is also designed to decrease harsh expressions of negative emotions such as criticism or hostility.

When combined with medication, FFT is helpful for reducing depression symptoms and increasing the ability to take medications as prescribed (Miklowitz et al. 2003). FFT can be helpful even if you participate in only a few sessions. Researchers have found that as few as two FFT sessions help increase family members' positive communication, and that this helps improve mood in the person with the diagnosis (Simoneau et al. 1999). Combined with medication, improving the way your family functions appears to be one way to decrease symptoms of bipolar disorder and prolong wellness.

Interpersonal and Social Rhythm Therapy

Another approach to staying healthy is to decrease behaviors or experiences that may make symptoms more likely to occur. Interpersonal and social rhythm therapy (IPSRT) focuses on reducing risk factors that could contribute to relapse. For example, there is strong evidence that sleep deprivation can trigger manic symptoms (Colombo et al. 1999). There is also good evidence that stress and interpersonal conflict can trigger depressive symptoms for a person with bipolar disorder (Johnson 2005a). In IPSRT, you learn strategies for reducing these risk factors. Research shows that when IPSRT is combined with medication, it is helpful for decreasing symptoms of depression and preventing future depressive episodes (Miklowitz et al. 2003; Frank et al. 2005).

IPSRT is designed to address the disruption to circadian rhythms that commonly occurs in bipolar disorder. Circadian rhythms are the internal biological cycles that regulate many of the body's daily processes, such as sleeping and waking. IPSRT includes strategies to help you recognize events that can disrupt your schedule, such as traveling to another time zone, doing shift work, or not having a regular daily routine. Stress and changes in relationships can also disrupt schedules and sleep. IPSRT focuses on helping you develop a regular routine for important activities like sleeping, eating, taking your medications, and exercising, and this can aid in preventing relapses. To that end, an IPSRT therapist might work with you to record and improve your sleep habits and daily routines.

A second set of skills in IPSRT involves identifying key stressors and social difficulties and working to improve those areas of your life. In IPSRT, you might choose one or two central sources of stress and work with your therapist to come up with a game plan for addressing them.

Interpersonal and Social Rhythm Therapy Model

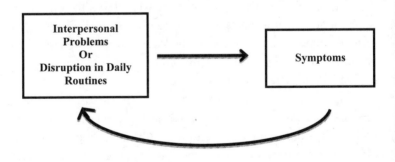

OTHER APPROACHES TO TREATING BIPOLAR DISORDER

While the treatments we just reviewed are the most commonly recommended—in combination with medication—there are other strategies. However, these have less research supporting their effectiveness in treating bipolar disorder. When deciding on the right treatment plan, it's important that you sort through your options carefully and even critically, weighing the pros and cons of each option with your treatment team.

Support Groups

It can be comforting to interact with other people who have a diagnosis of bipolar disorder. No one knows more about this illness than others who have experienced the same ups and downs. Joining a support group can help you connect with people who have had similar experiences, enhance your ability to stay well in times of stress, and give you the opportunity to both give and receive support. Support groups provide a great outlet to share symptoms, struggles, and accomplishments with a community of people who understand your experiences.

Support groups are usually organized by treatment facilities or consumer groups and are available in person and online for both individuals and their families. Although support groups offer the opportunity to meet new people and create new friendships, they aren't for everybody. Some people find that it can be overwhelming to hear about other people's difficulties with the disorder. If you find that for any reason you aren't comfortable in a given group, you may want to try other support groups in your area to find a group you feel comfortable with. The atmosphere, level of positivity, and style of different support groups can vary widely. Also, be aware that although confidentiality is expected, it isn't guaranteed in a support group, so you may want to be careful about how much personal information you share. A great resource for finding local and online support groups is the Depression and Bipolar Support Alliance website (under the Find Support link at www.dbsalliance.org).

Spirituality and Religion

While faith and prayer are comforting for people with a large range of health problems, there is no evidence that they are as effective for treating bipolar disorder as medications or the psychosocial treatments we reviewed in this chapter. Spiritual practices may be a helpful addition to other treatments, but they are not as effective by themselves.

Exercise

Regular exercise can help all people maintain a healthy lifestyle. However, it is important for people with bipolar disorder to regulate their exercise routines so they don't get overenergized or excessively goal-driven, and so exercise doesn't interfere with sleep. The best way to incorporate exercise into your life is to make sure you exercise for short periods on a regular schedule, and that you do so fairly early in the day.

Diet and Vitamins

While there appears to be a lower rate of bipolar disorder in countries with higher fish consumption (Noaghiul and Hibbeln 2003), there is no evidence that supplementing with omega-3 fatty acids (which are abundant in seafood) has any impact on symptoms or relapse. Furthermore, taking vitamins or other nutritional supplements isn't likely to be as beneficial if this isn't accompanied by other lifestyle changes, such as getting enough sleep, eating healthful food, and exercising.

DECIDING WHICH TREATMENT IS BEST FOR YOU

So now that you know more about effective treatments for bipolar disorder, how do you decide which is best for you? Research comparing cognitive behavioral therapy, family-focused therapy, and interpersonal and social rhythm therapy found that, when combined with medication, any of these therapies help speed recovery from bipolar depression and prevent future episodes (Miklowitz et al. 2007). All of these therapies appear to be equally effective when used in combination with medication. Additionally, therapy lasting several months helps more than psychoeducation lasting a few weeks.

There are a number of important characteristics that all of the psychosocial treatments we've reviewed here have in common. First, research supports the effectiveness of all of these interventions for treating bipolar disorder when combined with medication. Second, each treatment includes education about the disorder, either for those with bipolar disorder individually or as part of a group, or for family members. Third, all of these treatments help people identify, track, and prevent symptoms and future episodes. Lastly, these interventions all assist people in creating and maintaining more regular routines and patterns of behavior. Thus, psychosocial treatments can be very useful in helping you learn more about bipolar disorder and providing tools you can use to stay healthy.

When choosing which route to take, it's important to think carefully about which treatment is the best fit for you. If your diagnosis is fairly new or you feel you don't know very much about bipolar disorder, you might want to start with a psychoeducation program. Then, depending on what your goals are, you may prefer one type of therapy to another. For instance, it may help to think about whether you're experiencing difficulty with negative thinking (in which case CBT might be best), family conflict (in which case FFT might be best), or interpersonal problems or disruptions in your daily routines (in which case IPSRT might be best). Also consider which symptoms are most problematic for you—depression or mania. (If mania is more problematic for you, IPSRT would probably be your last choice.) Be sure to discuss your options and preferences with your treatment team so you can work together to come up with the best plan to help you take care of yourself. The summary below may help you think through these factors when choosing a psychosocial treatment.

SUMMARY OF PSYCHOSOCIAL TREATMENTS THAT WORK

Treatment: Psychoeducation

Who participates?

People with bipolar disorder (one-on-one or in a group) or family members

Some knowledge and skills you'll learn

- What bipolar disorder is and how it is diagnosed
- How to recognize symptoms of mania and depression
- Ways to track early warning signs
- What to do in case of an emergency

Most helpful for symptoms of...

Mania and depression

You may want to consider this if you...

Want to learn more about what bipolar disorder is and how to recognize and respond to symptoms

Treatment: Cognitive Behavioral Therapy (CBT)

Who participates?

People with bipolar disorder

Some skills you'll learn

- How to identify patterns in thinking, feeling, and behaving

- Ways to identify and change negative thought patterns

- Ways to decrease overly positive thinking in mania

Most helpful for symptoms of…

Depression, and can also help with symptoms of mania

You may want to consider this if you…

Tend to have overly negative thinking or want to understand how your thoughts, feelings, and behaviors are connected

Treatment: Family-Focused Therapy (FFT)

Who participates?

People with bipolar disorder and their family members

Some skills you'll learn

- How to improve family communication styles

- How to identify and solve family conflicts

- Strategies to decrease expression of negative emotions

Most helpful for symptoms of…

Depression, and can also help with symptoms of mania

You may want to consider this if you…

Want to resolve family conflicts or work on communication with family members

Treatment: Interpersonal and Social Rhythm Therapy (IPSRT)

Who participates?

People with bipolar disorder

Some skills you will learn

- Ways to reduce stress

- How to ensure you take your medication regularly

- How to improve relationships with others

- Strategies to maintain regular daily routines, including sleeping, waking, eating, and exercising

Most helpful for symptoms of...

Depression

You may want to consider this if you...

Have difficulty maintaining a regular schedule or have interpersonal difficulties

WHAT TO EXPECT IN PSYCHOTHERAPY

Once you decide which type of psychotherapy is the best fit for you, you may wonder what the experience will be like. If you've never been in therapy before, it can understandably be overwhelming at first. Most therapies involve meeting with a therapist once a week, but this varies depending on the severity of your symptoms and how you're doing at a particular time. Sessions usually last about fifty minutes, but again, this may vary depending on your goals and level of distress. Most therapies are designed to be short-term, meaning that treatment will probably last twelve to sixteen weeks.

Something important to remember about psychotherapy is that you tend to get out of it what you put into it. The more you open yourself up to the process and to working collaboratively with your therapist, the more you will benefit from the tools and strategies you learn. Just as importantly, if you aren't comfortable with the type of therapy you're receiving or if you have questions about your treatment, you should always discuss your concerns with your therapist or other members of your treatment team. You will benefit the most from psychosocial interventions when you have strong and open communication with your care providers about your progress, how you're feeling, and, of course, any symptoms you're experiencing.

Most people feel a bit intimidated about asking therapists questions, particularly when meeting them for the first time. As discussed in chapter 2, it's reasonable to ask questions, including how much experience therapists have with treating bipolar disorder and which of the treatments for bipolar disorder they feel comfortable offering. That said, what's most important is to find someone you'll feel comfortable talking with about difficult experiences.

Some people simply feel uncomfortable about seeking therapy. They worry that it's a sign of weakness, or that somehow they should be able to conquer mental health issues on their own. However, mania and depression are very hard experiences to come to terms with, and restoring your sense of confidence in yourself after an episode can be a challenge. Having a therapist is like having a coach who offers support in that process and helps you rebuild parts of your life that might have been damaged by symptoms. Therefore, it isn't surprising that people who seek effective therapy for their bipolar symptoms tend to feel better about their life and stay well for longer periods.

SUMMARY

There are several effective psychosocial treatments that can be helpful for bipolar disorder. Choosing the treatment or treatments that are best for you or your family may depend on which aspects of your life you most want to improve. Another factor is whether you would prefer to work with a therapist individually or in a group setting. Work with your treatment team to decide which options best fit your goals.

CHAPTER 5

LEARNING TO NOTICE EARLY WARNING SIGNS AND TRIGGERS

Noticing changes in your mood or behaviors can help protect you from future mood episodes. For example, you may notice that you don't want to spend time with family or friends or that you're getting into arguments with strangers for no reason. Events like these may indicate that your mood is beginning to get too low or too high. The earlier you notice these changes, the more time you have to protect yourself from experiencing additional or more intense symptoms in the future. In this chapter, we'll review changes in your emotions, behaviors, and thoughts that may occur before mood episodes (warning signs), as well as life events that may increase your risk for an episode (triggers). In the next chapter, we'll talk about strategies to implement when you notice these early warning signs and triggers.

WARNING SIGNS

Before you become depressed, manic, or hypomanic, you may experience behaviors, thoughts, or emotions that act as clues, telling you that your mood is going up or down. We call these *warning signs*.

Common warning signs of depression

- Lower self-esteem

- Social isolation

- A drop in academic or job performance

- Problems with memory or attention

- Feeling fatigued

- Enjoying activities less

- Worrying more

- Talking less than usual

- Neglecting important activities

- Apathy or feeling indifferent

Common warning signs of mania or hypomania

- Sleeping less
- Feeling impatient
- Feeling irritable
- Having more energy
- Talking faster or more frequently than usual
- Driving faster
- Starting many new projects at once
- Feeling more confident
- Changing the way you dress
- Experiencing increased sexual feelings

These are just examples, and each person's warning signs may be different. Even for a given person, the warning signs may change from one mood episode to the next. As you can see, warning signs can be symptoms of depression, mania, or hypomania. As explained in chapter 1, you must experience a certain number of symptoms for a certain amount of time for the term "mood episode" to apply. However, symptoms that occur before an actual episode of mania or depression may be warning signs that you are moving toward relapse, and noticing these warning signs can help you take action to stay well.

People often wonder how they can tell the difference between normal changes in mood and warning signs. The basic difference is that normal mood swings tend to disappear after a few hours. An example would be getting into an argument with a friend and feeling down for the afternoon, but feeling better and moving on to thinking about other things by the end of the day. The warning signs of a mood episode, on the other hand, tend to get worse over time. For example, after that argument with a friend, you feel low for several days, start to isolate yourself from your friends, and begin experiencing changes in your appetite and sleep.

TRIGGERS

Equally as important as identifying warning signs is thinking about what causes those warning signs to occur. Sometimes things that happen in your life, both good and bad, can influence your mood. These are called *triggers* because they may result in mood symptoms or an episode of mania or depression. Importantly, triggers tend to come before warning signs. So if you can identify your triggers, you can intervene even sooner, taking care of yourself and implementing strategies to prevent mood symptoms from arising or developing into another episode. Identifying triggers is particularly important with mania and hypomania, because the time it takes to go from having only a few symptoms to experiencing a full-on episode can be just a few hours or days, rather than the days or weeks it may take with depression. As with warning signs, each person can have different triggers.

The Links Between Triggers, Warning Signs, and Risks

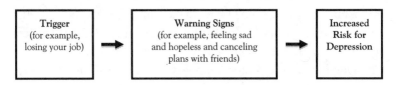

Identifying your triggers can help you ward off symptoms and feel more in control of your illness. Here are some common triggers people with bipolar disorder report. When reading this section, think about whether these may be triggers for you and whether you can identify any others.

Stress. Major life stressors and experiences, whether good or bad, are often triggers for symptoms. Common triggers for depression include losing friends or family members or losing a job. Common triggers for mania include receiving a promotion or experiencing a terrific social event, such as falling in love. Chronic stress, meaning stress that lasts a long time, can lead to both physical and psychological problems, including disruptions in sleep, changes in regular routines, or changes in mood, all of which can increase the risk of another mood episode.

Achieving goals. While negative life events can trigger depression, experiencing successes and having exciting new opportunities may lead to an increase in mania symptoms (Johnson et al.

2008). Although most people find it rewarding to reach their goals, research suggests that individuals with bipolar disorder may be more sensitive to rewarding experiences (Johnson 2005b). For example, people with bipolar disorder tend to place a higher importance on pursuing goals, even when they aren't experiencing a manic episode (Johnson, Eisner, and Carver 2009). This can lead to an escalating cycle in which achieving a goal triggers symptoms of mania, such as feeling overconfident, and then, when manic, you feel more impulsive and able to achieve anything you put your mind to. As a result, you may pursue several large projects at the same time, regardless of whether you have the resources to complete them. We don't advocate abandoning your goals; rather, we encourage you to be aware of changes in your confidence level, pace yourself, and choose realistic steps toward achieving your goals without taking too many risks.

Changes in sleep habits. Changes to your normal sleep schedule, including getting significantly fewer hours of sleep than usual, can trigger episodes of mania (Barbini et al. 1998). For example, pulling all-nighters or getting only a few hours of sleep for two nights in a row may be enough to trigger a manic episode for some individuals. In addition, sleep regulates dopamine receptors in the brain, and as mentioned in chapter 1, dopamine is a neurotransmitter that's related to emotions and pleasure. Having emotionally charged experiences just before bed, such as thinking about exciting events, can also disrupt sleep for people with bipolar disorder (Harvey, Talbot, and Gershon 2009).

Exercise. Although exercise can act as a natural antidepressant, it also has stimulating properties that may trigger mania if it interferes with your sleep or dominates your daily activities. We recommend that you exercise regularly and schedule your workouts during the morning or early afternoon. Exercising late in the day may keep you awake longer and interfere with your ability to get a good night's sleep on your regular schedule. It may also lead to excessive goal-driven behavior.

Drugs and alcohol. Many people with bipolar disorder find themselves drawn toward using drugs to help regulate their moods and sleep. Often, this ends up backfiring and people find it difficult to control their drug use. Generally, drugs that make you feel more energetic or that interfere with your sleep carry a major risk of triggering an episode of mania. For example, powerful stimulants like cocaine or speed and some hallucinogens, such as LSD, increase your energy level and decrease your need for sleep, which can overwhelm your body's ability to regulate your mood and sleep. With substances that tend to have more calming effects, such as barbiturates or alcohol, you run the risk of triggering depression with repeated use. In addition, many nonprescription drugs can interfere with prescription medications, which may lead to unanticipated side effects. If you're finding it hard to manage your use of any drugs, seek professional help so you can learn alternative ways of coping. In addition, you should always discuss any drug or alcohol use with your treatment team.

Caffeine. Caffeine is another substance that may disrupt your daily routine and sleep schedule and trigger changes in your energy level and mood. It's best to limit your consumption of food and drinks containing caffeine, including coffee, energy drinks, and some multivitamins. Some individuals are more sensitive to the effects of caffeine than others, and if you find you tend to become very energized from caffeine, don't underestimate the impact of a late-night soda, a piece of chocolate, or even a cup of green tea.

THE IMPORTANCE OF BEING AWARE OF SYMPTOMS

It's important to notice triggers and warning signs as early as possible. The more intense your symptoms are or the more symptoms you experience, the less able you are to recognize that you may need help or take the necessary steps to get support. Having insight into your symptoms is particularly important with mania and hypomania. In mania, as you experience more symptoms, your awareness of your symptoms decreases, so you'll have more trouble seeing that you're becoming manic and that you need to get help.

Sometimes people enjoy feeling hypomanic and want the feeling to last longer. However, it's important to recognize that hypomania can be like skating on thin ice. Chances are, your mood will continue to climb. The longer you wait to try to balance your mood, the harder it will be to recover from your symptoms. This may sound scary. However, by identifying triggers and early warning signs, you give yourself the opportunity to intervene on your own behalf before your insight decreases so much that you're unaware that you need support.

IDENTIFYING WARNING SIGNS AND TRIGGERS

In this section, we provide some strategies to help you identify your warning signs and triggers by looking for patterns in your moods and experiences. Keep in mind that this can be a challenging task, and it may take some time to get into the habit of practicing these strategies. However, the more you learn about yourself and your experiences with bipolar disorder, the easier it will be to notice changes in your mood, thoughts, and behavior. In chapter 6, we'll talk about what to do once you recognize warning signs or see that you're experiencing triggers.

Make a List

Some people find it helpful to make a list of their warning signs and triggers. There are many ways to create your list. One way is to think about whether you tend to have certain symptoms or experiences before an episode. To do so, it's often easiest to think about your most recent episode and work your way backward. For example, you may recollect that before your most recent depressive episode, you were really stressed at work. Or you might look back at your most recent manic episode and realize that, at the very outset, you started spending excessive amounts of money.

Noticing patterns in your routine can be another helpful way to track when your mood is becoming too low or too high. Ask yourself, *What am I doing today?* For example, when you're feeling sad, you may notice that you have trouble completing your usual tasks: The dishes are stacking up, your to-do list only gets longer, and you cancel plans with friends. Not having any plans for the day could be a warning sign that you need to take care of yourself by scheduling some small events that are rewarding or pleasant. On the other hand, with mania you may find that every minute of the day is filled. For example, you might feel too busy to take lunch breaks because you have so many things you want to do. Getting too busy or overly engaged with projects can be a warning sign of mania, and if you notice this happening, you can use the insight to try to work on one goal at a time.

Here's an example of a list of warning signs and triggers.

Sarah's Warning Signs for Mania

1. *Great mood, feeling on top of the world*

2. *Sleeping less than 6 hours a night*

3. *Spending more than $300 a week on things I don't need and can't afford*

4. *Thinking people are frustrating and too slow*

5. *Others seeing me as moving too fast and being too enthusiastic about my projects*

Sarah's Triggers for Mania and Hypomania

1. *Staying up late and not getting enough sleep*

2. *Drinking caffeinated beverages*

3. *Completing a big project at work*

Ask Others for Help

Another strategy for figuring out patterns in your history is to enlist the help of close family members, trusted friends, and your treatment team to see what changes they've noticed when you've started to feel too high or too low in the past. For example, your friends may help you see that you tend to become more talkative when moving toward a manic episode because they've noticed that they can't get a word in edgewise during those times. They may comment that this tends to happen when you are working long hours. Or perhaps your family might help you see that you enjoy your favorite activities less when you start to become depressed, and that this tends to happen when you don't see friends on a regular basis. Getting others' input can help you make sure you don't forget any important warning signs or triggers when you make your list. In addition, it may be comforting to talk with trusted friends and family members about what role they might play in helping you stay well.

Use a Daily Mood Chart

One useful strategy for identifying mood patterns is to use a *daily mood chart* to track changes in your mood day to day. There are many free online tools you can use to do this. For example, http://moodtracker.com has a helpful worksheet to record how you feel each day. It allows you to graph when you're feeling high or low, how much sleep you're getting, and any changes in your medications. The Depression and Bipolar Support Alliance (DBSA) has a website (www.facingus.org) featuring a mood charting tool that allows you to record even more daily and weekly details, such as changes in your lifestyle or health. It's called the Wellness Tracker and can be accessed through the Tour or Resources links. A similar charting tool can be found at www.healthyplace.com (under Tools); it's called the Mood Journal. Another site, www.moodscope.com, helps you track your moods through a simple card game you play each day.

Mood tracking can help you identify your warning signs and triggers. When tracking indicates that your mood is getting higher or lower, you can make a list of what's going on for you, such as situations or times that have made you feel better or worse. With time, you may be able to identify warning signs and triggers that consistently occur for you before an episode, pointing out the kinds of occurrences you should pay particular attention to in the future. Mood charts are also a good way to communicate your experiences or progress to your treatment team.

The Depression and Bipolar Support Alliance Facing Us website also has an online Wellness Plan tool that helps you compile personalized lists of warning signs and triggers and a crisis plan. If you prefer to use a book instead of an online tool, you may want to consider *The Bipolar Workbook: Tools for Controlling Your Mood Swings*, by Monica Ramirez Basco, or some of the other books listed in the Resources section at the back of the book.

In a typical mood chart, you'd list your prescribed medications and indicate whether you took them as scheduled. You can also note whether your mood is high or low, how much sleep you've gotten the night before, and whether you're using any substances. In addition, it's a good idea to list your daily activities and make notes about anything else that seems to have a bearing on your mood. Space doesn't permit us to include a full mood chart here; however, we've provided a streamlined version that you can use if you'd like to create your own mood tracking chart. This is just an example, and over time, you may find other ways to customize your daily mood chart.

Weekly Mood Chart		1	2	3	4	5	6	7
Dates:								
Day of the Week		1	2	3	4	5	6	7
Med 1:								
Med 2:								
Med 3:								
High Mood	Severe							
	Moderate							
	Mild							
Low Mood	Mild							
	Moderate							
	Severe							
Hours of Sleep								
Anxiety (rate 0 to 10)								
Irritability (rate 0 to 10)								
Alcohol or drug use?								

Work on a Life Chart

Understanding patterns in your mood is a work in progress, not something that can be done in one sitting. While it can help to record your daily moods and behaviors, it's also helpful to track the history of your symptoms in earlier years. By looking for patterns involved in your previous mood episodes, you can increase your understanding of your mood. While similar to keeping a mood chart on a day-to-day basis, this approach, known as *life charting*, involves thinking about mood episodes in hindsight and recording details of your experience over the years, such as the different symptoms you've experienced, when they occurred, how severe they were, how often they occurred, which treatments were effective at treating them, and what potential triggering events transpired before the onset of symptoms. This technique can help you keep a thorough record of your mood history across your life.

Because it involves thinking about multiple episodes of mood disturbance and a longer history, life charting is best done in collaboration with your treatment team. It can help both you and your treatment team notice patterns in your mood over time and help guide decisions about your treatment. Bipolar Network News (bipolarnews.org), an online clearinghouse for information on mood disorders, has a thorough description of life charting for both past and current events that is accessible through the Life Charts link. As with mood charts, you can design your own system for keeping track of your mood episodes and periods of wellness depending on what works best for you. Here's an example of what a completed life chart might look like.

	Aug 2004 to Oct 2004	March 2005 to July 2005	Oct 2006 to Feb 2007
Severe Mania			
Moderate Mania			
Mild Mania			
Mild Depression			
Moderate Depression			
Severe Depression			
Life Events	Started school and moved from home	Took leave from school	Returned to school, stopped lithium
Medication	Lithium	Lithium	Depakote
School/Job	New school	Semester off	New coursework

SUMMARY

Detecting changes in your mood in a timely way is crucial to avoiding an episode. Noticing small changes in your emotions, behaviors, and thoughts can allow you to quickly take steps to intervene on your own behalf and stay healthy. The triggers that lead to episodes and the point at which it's important to take action differ from person to person. The best thing to do when you're experiencing symptoms is to notify your treatment team so you can work together to make a decision about the best steps to help you stay well. In chapter 6, we'll provide strategies for responding to warning signs and triggers once you notice them, for coping with changes in your mood and behavior, and for creating a plan in case your mood becomes more extreme.

CHAPTER 6

STRATEGIES FOR
RESPONDING TO
WARNING SIGNS
AND TRIGGERS

As discussed in chapter 5, noticing changes in your mood, behavior, or thoughts as early as possible can help you stay well. These changes, or warning signs, are reminders to take care of yourself and get additional support. Sometimes it can be hard to know if the warning signs you're experiencing need to be treated, and if so, how. When you begin to notice warning signs or simply aren't feeling like yourself, a good first step is to get in touch with your treatment team so they can give you their opinion on whether it would be helpful to increase your support or focus on coping skills.

In this chapter, we'll discuss what to do if you notice your mood is getting too high or too low, including strategies to help you balance your mood and techniques for prolonging wellness. Research has found that people with bipolar disorder are able to recognize when they're experiencing warning signs of depression and mania, that they can use this information to implement strategies for balancing their mood, and that doing so benefits their well-being (Lam and Wong 1997). This chapter will help you do the same.

STRATEGIES FOR RESPONDING TO WARNING SIGNS OF MANIA

In chapter 5, we discussed ways to identify symptoms of mania as part of a strategy to help prevent relapse, but once you notice them, what can you do? Thinking ahead and identifying strategies you will use when you notice that you're getting irritable or your mood is getting high can help you get the support you need and increase your chances of remaining well. There are three main types of strategies: self-calming, self-protection, and managing medications and other treatments.

Self-Calming Strategies

Strategies to help you feel calm and relaxed can help balance your mood when you start to feel hypomanic or manic. Here are some things you can try:

- Increase the number of hours you sleep to a minimum of ten. Before the development of current medications for bipolar disorder, sleeping was actually one of the main treatments for mania. In fact, sleeping for a long time for three or four days in a row can be enough to restore mood and prevent relapse. If you can't fall asleep, resting quietly without TV, radio, or other distractions in a quiet room can still be restorative.

- Limit the number of activities and tasks you're doing. Remember that avoiding relapse is more important than a work obligation or social commitment. If you have difficulty scaling back, try to prioritize your activities as soon as you notice that your mood is getting higher, then focus only on what is most important.

- Spend no more than six hours a day being active, and try to spend the rest of the day resting and relaxing, seeking as much tranquility as you can find and limiting your outings.

- Don't try to subdue increased energy with efforts to exhaust yourself with exercise or more activity. The more active you are, the more stimulated you'll become and the more energetic you'll feel. As mentioned in chapter 5, when you feel manic or hypomanic, exercise is recommended only if it is gentle and controlled, doesn't interfere with sleep, and doesn't become excessive or intensify your energetic state.

- Reduce stimulation. For example, avoid places or situations that you find highly energizing, such as shopping centers, crowded parties, or romantic situations. Instead, choose a relaxing environment—somewhere quiet, with low light and few people.

- Avoid food and beverages containing stimulants, such as coffee, tea, soda, and energy drinks; multivitamins and over-the-counter medications sometimes contain caffeine too. Also avoid alcohol and stimulating drugs. Even if you're able to limit your alcohol consumption, it's best to not drink at all if you start to notice symptoms.

- Engage in calming activities, such as taking a walk, doing deep breathing or yoga, or meditating. Even something like sitting in a rocking chair and listening to relaxing music or being around calm people can help steady your mood.

- Have a go-to list of a few small actions you can take to slow yourself down, like sitting in the sun for ten minutes or calling a friend who you find soothing.

Self-Protection Strategies

After a manic or hypomanic episode, people sometimes find that they've done things that make their recovery more difficult, such as spending more money than they have or making major decisions without thinking them through. Here are some strategies you can put into place ahead of time to make it easier to prevent these kinds of outcomes if your warning signs or symptoms become more severe:

- If you notice symptoms of mania or any of your warning signs, limit your spending. You can ask your credit card company to lower your credit limit or ask a trusted friend to hold on to your credit cards—especially if you notice that you feel like going on a shopping spree. As mentioned in chapter 4, some people freeze their credit cards in ice to help them postpone making purchases for at least twenty-four hours. This can give you time to think about your decision before spending.

- Postpone making any big decisions until after you've spoken with your treatment team or a supportive friend or family member. For example, don't start a new business or a political venture while your mood is high. Have a rule that you'll sit on any major decision for twenty-four hours to give yourself time to weigh the pros and cons. If an opportunity is truly a good fit for you, it's likely that you can still pursue it later, when you're feeling calmer.

- Don't give yourself permission to feel high "a little longer." Remember, the higher you go, the harder you'll fall. The sooner you can reduce symptoms of hypomania or mania, the less likely it is that these symptoms will progress into a manic episode.

- Talk to someone you know well and trust to get some perspective on your experience. Others may be able to help you determine whether your behavior is out of the ordinary.

- In general, try not to act impulsively or put yourself in situations where you could endanger yourself. Avoid new flirtations and romances and unsafe sex. Stay away from conflicts and conflictual situations. If you're tempted to speed when your mood is high, don't drive. Avoid high-pressure social situations, such as public speaking engagements.

Managing Medications and Other Treatments

Don't stop taking your medications when you experience symptoms, particularly when you're feeling energized and confident. As mentioned in chapter 3, it's common for people to think they don't need their medications when they're hypomanic or manic. When you notice changes in your mood, it may be helpful to consult with your psychiatrist to see if it would be appropriate to increase or change your medications. Sometimes an adjust-ment to your medications can make a big difference in whether your warning signs develop into a manic episode. Don't adjust your dosages or make any other medication changes without the guidance of your doctor. If you're receiving treatment from a ther-apist, it may help to increase the number of times you meet for a while or to move your appointment to an earlier day or time of day. Some therapists may even offer a check-in over the phone.

STRATEGIES FOR RESPONDING TO WARNING SIGNS OF DEPRESSION

Just as with mania and hypomania, it's good to think ahead and plan some strategies for balancing your mood when you start feel-ing low. Once you begin feeling depressed, it can be hard to moti-vate yourself to take action, making it especially important to identify these strategies in advance. We have four primary recom-mendations here: doing things that usually make you feel good, exercising, taking advantage of your social support system, and challenging negative self-talk.

Doing Things That Usually Make You Feel Good

When you're feeling low, it's often hard to find the energy or motivation to do the things you usually like to do. However, staying active and engaged with others can help boost your mood and keep a low mood from getting worse. While it can be difficult to find the energy to do daily tasks, people often find that they feel better once they get moving. Think about the experiences that usually make you feel good, particularly when you're feeling sad or low. Make a list of them that you keep handy, and add to your list whenever new ideas come to you. Include a wide variety of activities, from simple to more ambitious. Then, when you're feeling low, plan out your day, actually writing your schedule down and being sure to include time for these pleasurable activities. If it seems hard to gather the energy and motivation to do something major, do something small off your list, such as walking around the block, taking a hot bath, or calling a fun friend. If holding a conversation with another person feels too taxing, going to a café or the movies and simply being around other people may be enough to help boost your mood. Don't wait until you feel motivated to start these activities. Accomplishing even the smallest task or doing something that might help lift your mood even a bit will help you begin to feel more motivated.

Exercising

As we mentioned in chapter 5, exercise acts a natural antidepressant (Dunn et al. 2005) and can be a good mood booster when you're feeling low. Getting a workout in, however small, can lift your mood and help you feel more motivated to interact with others or complete tasks. For example, you can take your dog for a walk or do some light stretching. Planning to exercise with a friend may help increase your motivation when you feel tired or want to isolate yourself.

Taking Advantage of Your Social Support System

Social support is a key ingredient in staying happy and healthy. Social isolation is a common warning sign of depression. If you find that you want to avoid interacting with others, that might serve as a gentle reminder that it's an important time to do the opposite and reach out. Getting some support can help you feel more connected to others and less alone in dealing with your problems. Talking to your therapist or a trusted friend or family member or attending a support group meeting can help boost your mood and help you make it through a low period. If leaving the house feels like too much, you can call someone supportive or invite a friend or family member to visit you. Problems can sometimes seem bigger than they are when you try to deal with them on your own. Talking through a problem with someone who cares about you can help reassure you and put your concerns into perspective.

Challenging Negative Self-Talk

When your mood is low, you're likely to feel bad about yourself or even feel hopeless. You may view yourself and the world in a negative light or feel like you don't have much control over your life. It's common to get into a cycle of feeling low, then not doing things you need or want to do because you feel tired or discouraged, and then feeling worse because you aren't able to get things done. If warning signs or symptoms of depression return, try not to beat yourself up. Instead, think about ways to actively work on feeling better and getting the support you need. Often, people who are depressed are much harsher toward themselves than they would be toward a friend, so listen to your self-talk and consider whether you'd be so critical of a friend who was struggling.

Remember that everyone experiences stress, and that occasionally having a hard time dealing with things is completely normal. Try not to fall into the trap of thinking you're back at square one when you feel stressed or overwhelmed. Everyone differs in terms of which situations are stressful for them, so we all have to come up with our own strategies for handling stress when it comes up. Try thinking about the resources you have for coping with a particular situation or reflecting on what's been helpful in the past. Remind yourself that most people have days when life is harder to handle. Setbacks are unfortunate, but they can help you learn something new about how to avoid similar problems in the future.

THE IMPORTANCE OF SLEEP

Since changes in sleep are known to trigger mood episodes, it's particularly important to maintain a regular sleep schedule. Seven to nine *consecutive* hours of sleep is the ideal for adults. Sleeping five hours at night and then taking a two-hour nap doesn't add up to seven hours of consecutive sleep. Also note that it's important to maintain your sleep schedule on the weekends. Sometimes you may stay up late for whatever reason. When this happens, try to stick to your schedule. It's better to wake up at your usual time than to sleep late to try to catch up on sleep. Sleeping in will just make it more difficult to fall asleep at your regular time the next night, making it more likely that you'll get stuck in this disrupted pattern.

Because good sleep habits can go a long way toward helping you stay well, we'll give you a number of tips for helping you keep a regular sleep schedule:

- Keep a sleep diary—a log to help you observe patterns in your sleep. This can also help you notice when warning signs or symptoms of mania or depression are starting, allowing you to take action as soon as possible. The National Sleep Foundation has a handy sleep diary you can use (search for "National Sleep Foundation sleep diary" in an Internet search engine).

- Identify how many hours you'll sleep, set a regular bedtime and awakening time, and try to keep to that schedule. Even if you feel like you can't sleep for seven to nine consecutive hours, give yourself all of those hours in one solid block for sleep or relaxation in a calm environment that helps quiet your mind. It's especially important to protect your routine during weekends, vacations, or travel.

- When you feel depressed, don't sleep or lie in bed any longer than seven to nine hours. If this is an issue, you may find it helpful to schedule activities or appointments in the morning so you have added motivation to get up and get going.

- Limit daytime naps to thirty minutes, and take a nap only if it won't interfere with your nighttime sleep.

- Limit your caffeine intake. This doesn't mean just coffee; don't underestimate the impact of a late-night caffeinated soda, chocolate dessert, or cup of tea.

- Avoid shift work and other activities that might disrupt your sleep schedule, such as late-night parties.

- Schedule in time to exercise—but not right before bedtime! Exercise can help you sleep more soundly. The best bet is to exercise in the morning or early afternoon.

Some people need extra support in managing their sleep routine. If you have trouble maintaining a consistent sleep schedule or find it difficult to fall asleep and stay asleep, talk to your treatment team about other methods for regulating your sleep. Psychiatrists can prescribe medications that can help, such as zaleplon (Sonata) or eszopiclone (Lunesta). These medications are usually prescribed to be taken as needed, also referred to as PRN, meaning you can take them on nights when falling asleep is especially challenging. Health professionals who specialize in treating sleep difficulties can help you learn additional skills for dealing with insomnia and regulating your sleep routine. For example, you might consider cognitive behavioral therapy for insomnia, a treatment that has been shown to have long-term benefits for people with insomnia (National Institutes of Health 2005). This type of therapy focuses on tracking your sleep patterns, helping you establish a regular sleep schedule, reducing inaccurate beliefs about sleep, and lowering anxiety related to sleep difficulties (Harvey 2008).

DEVELOPING A PLAN FOR MANAGING TRIGGERS

As discussed in chapter 5, triggers are things that happen in your life that may make it more likely that your mood will become imbalanced. Even positive events, like starting a new job or going on an exciting vacation, can be triggers. This doesn't mean you should avoid taking part in life's experiences and adventures, but it does mean it's worthwhile to identify your personal triggers. This can go a long way toward helping you know when you need to put extra effort into taking care of yourself.

Once you've identified your triggers, there are things you can do to prevent them from leading to an increase in symptoms, including some of the strategies we've discussed in this chapter. The first step is to make sure you have support and resources available to manage symptoms if they do occur. You should also consult with your treatment team whenever you experience changes in your life that may act as triggers, or ask trusted friends and family members to help provide support when you're going through a challenging experience.

For example, let's say Michelle is up for a promotion at work—a positive but stressful situation that may be a potential trigger. What can she do to make sure she remains in control? She can discuss the promotion with her treatment team, watch out for excessive focus on reaching her goals, and ask her family to tell her if they notice any warning signs (for example, they might say, "You seem really hyper and excited today. How's your sleep?").

Or let's say that Scott and his wife have a new baby on the way, which will create a lot of new responsibilities for him. What can he do to keep from feeling overwhelmed? He can increase his social support by reaching out to friends and family members ahead of time, and work with his treatment team to brainstorm coping strategies for when the baby comes. He might need to work out special arrangements so the baby doesn't interfere with getting solid sleep.

Anticipating potential events that may lead to changes in your mood and developing plans for managing these situations as they arise can help you feel more supported and decrease the chances of relapse.

REMEMBERING TO IMPLEMENT YOUR PLAN

We recommend developing a plan for responding to warning signs and triggers when you're feeling well. This will help you cope more effectively if symptoms return. Once you've come up with a plan, set yourself up for success by creating reminders, such as a wallet card or daily reminder card, so you can respond rapidly when triggers or warning signs occur.

Wallet Card

Use a wallet card to record contact numbers for your treatment team and the friends and family members who are most supportive, as well as the first three steps you'll take if your mood gets too high or too low. This can be an invaluable resource if you need immediate support. It can help you take control if symptoms emerge and help remind you of how to best ask for extra support. Like the list of warning signs discussed in chapter 5, the information on your wallet card may change over time. Here is an example of what the two sides of a wallet card might look like, along with a blank version you can copy, fill out, and carry with you.

THINGS TO DO IF SYMPTOMS RETURN

Psychiatrist: Dr. Mark Jones

Phone: 510-555-5555

Address: 123 Anywhere St.,
Berkeley, CA

Therapist: Dr. Jane Smith

Phone: 510-555-1234

Address: 234 Fictitious Dr.,
Berkeley, CA

Support

1. Michael Thomas

Phone: 510-555-4321

Address: 2988 Unknown Ave.,
Berkeley, CA

2. Carlos Law

Phone: 510-555-6789

Address: 336 Ersatz St., El
Cerrito, CA

3. Mollie Washington

Phone: 510-555-1111

Address: 73 Pseudo St.,
Oakland, CA

THINGS TO DO IF SYMPTOMS RETURN

When feeling high

1. Sit on big decisions for at least 24 hours!

2. Try to rest in a soothing place. Turn down the lights.

3. Give my credit cards to my brother.

What to say to friends/family: I'm feeling a little excited today and need to be in a calm environment.

When feeling low

1. Stick with my normal routine—don't keep sleeping.

2. Call a friend. Don't isolate myself!

3. Go to my support group.

What to say to friends/family: I'm feeling pretty down and need your support in staying connected.

If I can't get in touch with a support person or my symptoms continue, go to the nearest emergency room.

THINGS TO DO IF SYMPTOMS RETURN

Psychiatrist:

Phone:

Address:

Therapist:

Phone:

Address:

Support

1.

Phone:

Address:

2.

Phone:

Address:

3.

Phone:

Address:

THINGS TO DO IF SYMPTOMS RETURN

When feeling high

1.

2.

3.

What to say to friends/family:

When feeling low

1.

2.

3.

What to say to friends/family:

If I can't get in touch with a support person or my symptoms continue, go to the nearest emergency room.

Daily Reminder Card

It may help to set up a daily reminder to check your list of warning signs and triggers. This will help you carefully keep track of any symptoms so you can catch them as soon as they occur. We've included some blank examples of daily reminder cards (one for depression and one for mania or hypomania) so you can list both your warning signs and triggers and your strategies for dealing with them.

A daily reminder card is also a convenient place for you to write out how you'll communicate with friends and family members during times when your mood is high or low. You may find it helpful to put the card on your nightstand and just take a quick glance at it at the same time each day to see how you're doing. You can always revise the list if you notice new warning signs or triggers that are more meaningful or if you want to change the order of the list. You can photocopy the blank form we provide, or if you'd like more space, you can design something similar, in which case you might want to put the triggers and warning signs in one column and your planned coping strategies in another column alongside.

Depression Daily Reminder Card

Depression trigger or warning sign 1: _____

What I will do: _____

Depression trigger or warning sign 2: _____

What I will do: _____

Depression trigger or warning sign 3: _____

What I will do: _____

Depression trigger or warning sign 4: _____

What I will do: _____

Depression trigger or warning sign 5: _____

What I will do: _____

Depression trigger or warning sign 6: _____

What I will do: _____

Depression trigger or warning sign 7: _____

What I will do: _____

Depression trigger or warning sign 8: _____

What I will do: _____

What I will say to friends/family: _____

_____

What friends/family will say to me: _____

_____

Mania Daily Reminder Card

Mania trigger or warning sign 1: _____

What I will do: _____

Mania trigger or warning sign 2: _____

What I will do: _____

Mania trigger or warning sign 3: _____

What I will do: _____

Mania trigger or warning sign 4: _____

What I will do: _____

Mania trigger or warning sign 5: _____

What I will do: _____

Mania trigger or warning sign 6: _____

What I will do: _____

Mania trigger or warning sign 7: _____

What I will do: _____

Mania trigger or warning sign 8: _____

What I will do: _____

What I will say to friends/family: _____

_____

What friends/family will say to me: _____

_____

SUMMARY

To stay well and prolong periods of wellness, you need to not only recognize when your mood is getting high or low, but also think through what you'll do when you notice these warning signs. In this chapter, we provided several strategies for responding to warning signs of mania and depression. We also discussed the importance of planning ahead and seeking increased support when potential triggers arise. Think about which strategies you'll use when you start to feel too high and how you can boost your mood and get moving if your mood starts getting low. These strategies can be helpful at any point when you experience symptoms, even when your symptoms have progressed and you're in a manic or depressive episode. Remember that involving your treatment team and trusted family members and friends in your plan can help you stay well by providing emotional support and helping you track your symptoms.

CHAPTER 7

TELLING OTHERS ABOUT YOUR ILLNESS

Taking the time to think about and plan how you'll talk about your illness with people who aren't mental health professionals can make a big difference in the response and support you receive. Although you are educated about your illness, others may, unfortunately, be influenced by myths and biases about bipolar disorder. Sharing your situation with others for the first time can be a delicate issue. In this chapter, we'll provide tips on deciding whom to tell about your diagnosis and help you develop a script for doing so. We'll also cover how to answer common questions that others may have about your illness and how to take an active role in obtaining help from others.

Deciding whom to share your diagnosis with is a complex and personal decision. You may have many questions: What if I tell someone and that person doesn't understand? Should I tell a new employer before or after I accept a job? What do I say to my children? There are no clear rules about whom to tell, but thinking through these questions ahead of time will allow you to weigh the pros and cons and determine who needs to know and why. Your treatment team can also be a helpful resource when making these decisions.

DECIDING WHOM TO TELL

As with medical conditions, such as heart disease or asthma, sharing details about your mental health isn't always necessary. You are in control of whom you tell and how much information you share. Depending on how well you know someone, you may feel more or less comfortable confiding in that person about your illness. Here are some key considerations that can help you decide who may be an appropriate and supportive person to talk to about your illness.

What Are Their Attitudes toward Mental Illness?

Assessing whether people are accepting and kind about mental illness can be a good first step in deciding if you want to share more about your experiences. Before telling people, you may want to test the waters by bringing up the topic of mental illness without personalizing it. For example, you could say something like "Did you see that special on television about bipolar disorder?" or "I read an interesting article on medications for treating bipolar disorder." People's responses to such questions or comments may give you clues about how open and knowledgeable they are about mental illness. If they are warm and accepting, you may want to share your diagnosis. If they are critical, make derogatory comments, or seem apprehensive, you may not want to share your diagnosis, or if it's important to do so, you may want to try educating them about bipolar disorder before sharing your personal experiences. Someone who isn't open to hearing the truth about bipolar disorder or who is unable to express empathy for people affected by mental illness may not be a good source of support, and therefore might not be a person to whom you want to disclose your diagnosis.

What Will Sharing Your Diagnosis Help You Achieve?

A good rule of thumb is to share your diagnosis with people who will be supportive and understanding. If telling someone about your illness will provide you with extra support, then it's probably a good idea to open up about your experiences. When meeting new people, however, it generally isn't a good idea to share your diagnosis, since you haven't established a close and supportive relationship.

If symptoms of your illness could affect your relationships with certain people, it may be important to provide them with information about your situation. For example, knowing about your diagnosis may help your parents understand why you've missed several family events or help your partner understand why you're more irritable and impatient at times.

Identifying the Pros and Cons of Sharing

If you decide that someone is accepting of mental illness and will be supportive of you, the next step is to think about the pros and cons of sharing aspects of your illness with that particular person. Make a list of the benefits you anticipate and a list of the potential costs so you can more objectively weigh them. Doing this can help you decide whether or not to share this information and increase your confidence if you decide to do so. Let's take a look at some examples of common benefits and concerns.

BENEFITS OF SHARING

The benefits of disclosing your illness will differ depending on whom you're telling and what you're hoping to achieve. Here are some examples, but make sure the benefits you list are appropriate to your unique experiences, the person you're thinking of telling, and your relationship.

- *It will help explain some of my behaviors, such as why I sometimes become isolated or have trouble following through with plans.*

- *I can educate her about bipolar disorder so she'll better understand the illness and be less judgmental or afraid.*

- *She might not get as mad at me when I experience symptoms, like when I can't motivate myself to get out of bed.*

- *She can help me identify some of my warning signs and keep an eye out for triggers.*

- *I can lean on her for additional support.*

- *Being understood and accepted will feel good.*

- *I won't feel like I'm hiding a piece of myself anymore.*

POTENTIAL DOWNSIDES OF SHARING

It's understandable that you may have worries or doubts about how others will react when you share your diagnosis with them. In the following list of downsides, we've included some common concerns, but again, be sure you list your own worries and concerns and how likely they are to actually occur. That can help bring additional clarity to this important decision.

- *He may not understand.*

- *He may think I'm crazy or be afraid of me.*

- *He could judge me and think it's my fault that I have this disorder.*

- *He may not want to be my friend anymore.*

- *He may think I'm weak or fragile.*

- *He might think I'm unreliable or unpredictable.*

- *He may tell people who I don't want to know about my diagnosis.*

WEIGHING THE PROS AND CONS

After constructing your lists of pros and cons, take time to carefully weigh both sides. Pay particular attention to how many items you've come up with for each list and how much importance or weight each item holds. Thinking critically about both the benefits and the downsides of sharing your diagnosis with someone will help ensure that you make an informed and balanced decision.

DISCLOSURE SCRIPTS

Once you've made the decision to share your experiences of bipolar disorder with someone, it's important to think about the specific information you would like to share, how much detail to provide, and what you'll actually say. Creating a *disclosure script* can make it easier for you to talk about this difficult topic, ensure that you share only the necessary information, and help you if you forget what you want to say. The goal is to help others understand more about your illness in a way that will potentially increase your support and reduce their misconceptions about bipolar disorder. You may need to use different disclosure scripts with different people. When developing your disclosure script, it can be helpful to keep a few guidelines in mind.

Focus on the biological causes. People often don't realize that bipolar disorder is a biological disorder, just like cancer or heart disease. Focusing on the biological causes of the illness can help others understand that you aren't to blame for developing symptoms and that bipolar disorder is similar to other medical conditions. However, remember from chapter 1 that although biological factors can cause symptoms, symptoms aren't permanent and they can be treated. You'll probably want to share this as well.

Highlight the medical symptoms. Many people can more easily relate to the physiological symptoms of bipolar disorder, such as having trouble falling asleep or increased fatigue, because they've had similar experiences themselves. Focusing on these symptoms can help demystify bipolar disorder because it highlights common physiological experiences.

Use caution when discussing stigmatized symptoms. Some people with bipolar disorder experience symptoms such as suicidal thoughts, hallucinations, aggressive behavior, or hypersexuality. These more severe symptoms can seem scary or strange to people with limited knowledge about the disorder. Since these symptoms are often misunderstood, we suggest you not mention them when discussing your illness with someone for the first time. In general, it's best to discuss such symptoms only with your treatment team and close family members and friends.

Emphasize that you're being treated. Bipolar disorder and its effects on a person's life and behavior are often misunderstood. Although you know that there are helpful treatments that balance your mood and reduce symptoms, this may not be clear to everyone. Sharing that you're working closely with a treatment team to manage your illness and that many people with bipolar disorder can go years without symptoms tells others that your illness is under control and that you're actively prolonging your wellness. You might also stress that although bipolar disorder influences your behavior, it doesn't change who you are. Your illness is only one part of you, just like your hair color or family background; it doesn't define you.

Examples of Disclosure Scripts

Let's start with an example of what *not* to say (adapted from Colom and Vieta 2006): "I have a mental disorder that makes me lose control of my emotions and behaviors. Sometimes I may act really weird, and I have to go to the hospital until I'm normal again. Once I tried to kill myself. I take pills that the doctors tell me will help, but they make me feel like a zombie. My neighbor says that these pills are addictive, so sometimes I stop taking them until my symptoms come back." This example goes against the advice we shared above because it emphasizes a lack of control, shares dramatic or severe symptoms, reinforces the myth that bipolar medications are addictive, and doesn't focus on the steps you're taking to stay well.

Now let's look at a couple of examples of more helpful and positive disclosure scripts (adapted from Colom and Vieta 2006). Here's one approach you might use: "I have a medical illness called bipolar disorder that affects various systems in my body that help regulate mood. Sometimes I experience insomnia, anxiety, and restlessness, and once I had to be hospitalized. Other times, the disorder takes away all of my energy and makes me feel extremely tired, and I experience severe physical discomfort. Fortunately, I'm working with a treatment team and taking medications that help me a lot, though sometimes I may still experience symptoms or need extra support."

Here's another example of an effective approach: "I have a psychological disorder that's somewhat like many other medical conditions you may be familiar with, such as diabetes or a thyroid condition. It's called bipolar disorder. It's being treated and is under control, but I want to tell you so that you won't be surprised if I show symptoms. For example, I might have a lot of energy and have trouble sleeping, or I may feel really down and extremely tired and unmotivated. I take care of myself. Just like people with diabetes take insulin every day, I take medications, and sometimes I need adjustments to my medications, just like people who take thyroid medications or insulin. I am still the same person even though I have this diagnosis. It doesn't define who I am."

Compared to the first example, these two scripts are positive ways to talk about your illness because they emphasize biology and medicine, highlight that your symptoms are being treated and you're taking care of yourself, and communicate that your illness is under control. They also help others understand that one reason you're sharing this information is so they won't be surprised if you exhibit symptoms, and so they can be prepared to offer support if necessary.

Developing Your Own Disclosure Script

Now that you've seen some examples of disclosure scripts, take some time to think about how you'll tell other people about your illness. Remember that you may want to use different disclosure scripts with different people. Even so, the same general guidelines will apply in all cases. The point of a disclosure script isn't to hide aspects of your illness, but to provide clear information about the less stigmatizing aspects of your symptoms when telling others about your diagnosis for the first time.

After you initially share that you have bipolar disorder, tune in to the other person's reaction. Some people may have questions, while others may look at you blankly. Some will be supportive and understanding, while others may appear worried. Continue to educate yourself about your illness so you can answer questions, provide reassurance, and clarify any misconceptions others may have. Assessing whether others will be warm, accepting, and supportive is an ongoing process. Once you see a person's response to your initial disclosure, you can choose whether to share more details about your illness.

CHALLENGES WITH DISCLOSURE

Below are some common questions people ask about sharing their diagnosis with others. We've provided general information in response to each concern, but because everyone is unique and every situation is different, it's important to discuss your concerns with your treatment team. That way you can get information relative to your situation and receive the support you need.

Question: What if people judge me or don't understand?

Answer: It's common to have worries and concerns about what others will think of you once you disclose your illness. Although you are knowledgeable about the causes and best treatments for bipolar disorder, not everyone will be as informed. Sharing your knowledge is the best defense against judgment. Also know that there are some great resources to help people understand more. At the end of the book you'll find a Resources section that includes books designed for family and friends and autobiographies of people with bipolar disorder. Talking to your treatment team or a person you trust can also help you work through these concerns and help you cope if people are judgmental or unsupportive.

Question: Should I wait until I see symptoms before I tell others?

Answer: As discussed in chapter 5, there is always a risk with waiting until you notice symptoms to make decisions, get help, or start treatment. The more symptoms you experience, the less insight you may have that you need support. We recommend telling others about your diagnosis when you aren't currently experiencing symptoms. This makes it more likely that they'll be able to provide support if your symptoms return.

131

Question: Should I tell my children about bipolar disorder?

Answer: Telling children depends on their age. Explaining the details of any complicated medical condition can be confusing to children. There are children's books that help to explain bipolar disorder and address common concerns for a younger child (see the Resources section at the end of this book). If you decide your child is mature enough to learn more about your illness, you can develop a script, focusing on the medical or physical symptoms you experience. Then maintain an open and supportive dialogue so you can address any questions or concerns that come up. Because there's a genetic component to bipolar disorder, educating your children about your illness can also help them notice whether they experience symptoms and motivate them to learn skills for managing their moods. You may want to come up with a disclosure script to use with children with the advice and support of your treatment team. Some children may fear that they will develop the disorder; it is important for them to hear that most children who have a parent with bipolar disorder will not develop the disorder themselves.

Question: Should I tell people I'm dating or have just met?

Answer: Just because you have an illness doesn't mean it's the most important thing about you or that you need to share this information as soon as possible. Use the tips we provided earlier to test the waters and determine whether new people in your life are understanding and accepting about mental illness. Because bipolar disorder is a chronic illness, someone who isn't open to learning about it probably won't turn out to be a good fit for a long-term relationship. You'll know when the timing feels right. If you find yourself hiding or lying about your symptoms, it's probably time to make a decision about whether to share your diagnosis and how close you'd like the relationship to be.

Question: Should I tell my employer?

Answer: When deciding whether to tell your employer about your diagnosis, ask yourself, *Would I disclose my illness if it were some other medical condition, such as migraines or diabetes?* If not, it may not be necessary to disclose that you have bipolar disorder. If your symptoms affect your ability to fulfill your work requirements, however, you may want to talk to your employer to learn more about potential accommodations (for example, flexibility in your schedule and deadlines). If you're looking for a new job, you are not required by law to disclose your illness. However, we do recommend gathering information about aspects of the job that could trigger a future mood episode, such as shift work, stressful deadlines, or extended workdays. This may help you decide if it's in your best interest to pursue the position.

Question: What are my rights in the workplace?

Answer: The Americans with Disability Act (ADA) protects all people with physical or psychological disabilities against discrimination. Discrimination in the workplace includes denying people employment opportunities or promotions or not offering reasonable accommodations. However, in order to be protected under the ADA, you must disclose your illness to your employer. To learn more, visit the U.S. Equal Employment Opportunity Commission (eeoc.gov).

BEING OPEN TO EXTRA SUPPORT

Having conversations with others about the roles they'll play in your wellness helps you remain in control of when and how you receive support and also puts systems for receiving support in place before they're needed. It's human nature to feel hesitant to ask for help when times are tough. It's natural to think, *I've been through this before; I can get through it again on my own.* While it's great to have confidence in your abilities, the fact is, it's usually a lot easier to cope when you have the support of others.

There may also be times when you don't realize your symptoms have returned. At those times, it's helpful to have trusted friends, family members, or mental health professionals share their observations. Sometimes it can be difficult to hear what they have to say, especially if you don't believe your symptoms have returned. Talking to those you look to for support before you experience symptoms will help them learn more about how they can help, what to look for, and how to approach the topic so you'll be more willing to listen.

Developing a Support Agreement

Support agreements allow you to take an active role in the support you receive from others by detailing when you'd like support, how you'd like others to help, and what you'd like them to say to you when they notice warning signs. This can be especially useful if you go through times when you are not as aware of your symptoms or during times when you need some extra support.

Each support agreement will probably be different, depending on the person and your relationship. And although many people find this approach useful, it doesn't work for everyone; it depends on how comfortable you are with involving friends or family members in your treatment plan.

In all cases, be very specific. Include warning signs that the other person may notice that can serve as a signal that this is a time when you would like help. Also explain precisely how the person can help you best. Do you need a listening ear? Do you want advice? Do you want the other person to help you make decisions? Also think about the least threatening way the person can approach you during these times. What would you like to hear when the person notices warning signs?

The goal isn't to feel like your every move is being scrutinized, but to have a safety net so that others can be a voice of reason and support if you become less aware of your mood or behaviors or less able to use strategies to help balance your mood. Remember, the sooner you notice warning signs, the earlier you can act on your plans for coping and maintain wellness.

Example of a Support Agreement

Here's an example of a support agreement. We've also included a blank form you can use for writing support agreements. However, due to space constraints you may want to simply use the example as a model for your own form. Either way, identify someone you can count on for support, then work together to develop a support agreement.

135

MARIA'S SUPPORT AGREEMENT

Who: *Husband*

When I would like help: *When you notice that I charge more than four hundred dollars on nonessential items in one week, sleep less than five hours a night, or quickly jump to conclusions and start arguments.*

How you can help me: *Be patient if I start an argument, help me think through my purchases before I buy them, and, most importantly, help me keep my appointments with my therapist and psychiatrist.*

What I would like to hear: *It would be helpful if you could say something like "I'm noticing some of the warning signs we talked about, and I want you to know I'm here to help if you need me."*

MY SUPPORT AGREEMENT

Who:

When I would like help:

How you can help me:

What I would like to hear:

SUMMARY

Sharing information about your illness and symptoms can be a complicated endeavor. To help ensure that you receive the support and understanding you deserve, take the time to make careful decisions about whom to tell and how much detail to share. Think through the pros and cons of disclosing your diagnosis to a particular person to help you make a decision that feels right to you. If you decide to share your diagnosis, develop a disclosure script for the conversation. Sharing your diagnosis with trusted friends and family members will be beneficial, as it's often easier to cope with symptoms when you have the encouragement and understanding of others. Also remember that your treatment team can be a great source of support both when you're experiencing symptoms and when you're well.

CHAPTER 8

<hr>

STAYING WELL AND STAYING HOPEFUL

Once people are diagnosed with bipolar disorder, the focus on symptoms, mood management, and wellness tends to overshadow some of the good that comes with the diagnosis. One key benefit is that it opens the door to setting wellness goals for managing your illness and improving your general well-being. We begin our last chapter with some examples of wellness goals to get you started. We'll also briefly discuss some of the positive traits associated with bipolar disorder, including creativity, ambitiousness, and zest for life. We hope to leave you with a sense of hope, empowerment, and encouragement that will help you play an active role in shaping how this illness impacts your life.

SETTING WELLNESS GOALS

Receiving a diagnosis of bipolar disorder may feel devastating at first. However, it is actually the first step on your road to health. Now you can set wellness goals and decide which strategies and skills you'll need to use to reach them. Setting goals that are both realistic and meaningful can help you stay motivated during times when you're feeling down or recovering from an episode of mania or depression. Prioritizing your wellness goals and tracking your progress will help you stay conscious of the positive steps you're taking to stay healthy. Here are some examples of possible wellness goals.

Preventing relapse. Because bipolar disorder can be a chronic illness, one important goal is to prevent future episodes of mania or depression. While you may not be able to completely eliminate symptoms of the disorder, you can manage your symptoms and extend periods of wellness by using the strategies in this book.

Managing your medications. Becoming more informed about which medications work best for you, making it a priority to take your medications regularly, and talking to a professional before making changes or discontinuing your medication are important wellness goals that can maximize periods of balanced mood.

Feeling more in control. Educating yourself by using self-help resources like those mentioned in this book and listed in the Resources section can help empower you to manage your mood, work collaboratively with others to stay healthy, and feel more in control of your well-being. Staying involved in decisions about your care and having a plan in place for when symptoms arise can help you take responsibility for your wellness and increase your self-confidence that you can manage your triggers, notice warning signs, and cope with the inevitable difficulties in life.

Focusing on self-care. As you now know, tracking your symptoms, building social support, managing stress, establishing daily routines, getting enough sleep, exercising regularly (but not excessively!), and making time for relaxation are all helpful strategies for maintaining wellness. Additional self-care approaches include participating in the activities you enjoy, eating a healthful diet, connecting with supportive people, and making sure you stay centered. Working on these wellness goals will ensure that you're making your health and happiness a priority.

THE POSITIVE SIDE OF BIPOLAR DISORDER

The media often portrays people with bipolar disorder as being out of control or constantly experiencing symptoms. While this may be true for some individuals, many people with bipolar disorder have full and satisfying lives (Coryell et al. 1998). Even though many people struggle with this illness, about 25 percent of people with bipolar disorder report that their work and social lives are good or better, with as many as 15 percent describing their professional and personal abilities as "excellent" (Gitlin et al. 1995;

Hammen, Gitlin, and Altshuler 2000). Furthermore, when more than three thousand people with bipolar disorder were asked if they would press a button that would eliminate the disorder, about half said no, indicating that this illness has some positive aspects and that people with this diagnosis can live fulfilling lives (Wilson 2006).

Indeed, there is evidence that some people with bipolar disorder have exceptional qualities. Among the many notable people believed to have or have had the disorder are artists Vincent van Gogh, Edvard Munch, and Jackson Pollock; musicians Robert Schumann, Brian Wilson, and Sergei Rachmaninoff; actors Richard Dreyfuss, Carrie Fisher, Patty Duke, and Vivien Leigh; and authors Charles Dickens, Ernest Hemingway, Edgar Allen Poe, Virginia Woolf, William Faulkner, and F. Scott Fitzgerald. Other public figures who have talked about their experiences with bipolar disorder include Representative Patrick Kennedy and media personality Jane Pauley. More recently, celebrities such as Catherine Zeta-Jones and Russell Brand have disclosed that they were diagnosed with bipolar disorder, increasing public awareness and understanding of this illness. When times get tough, it can help to remember that you are not alone in experiencing symptoms and that people with bipolar disorder can have successful careers and lead fulfilling lives.

Researchers have found that people diagnosed with bipolar disorder exhibit a number of strengths (see Johnson et al. 2012 for a more thorough review), including higher creativity, higher lifetime ambition, and more motivation to pursue goals. Moreover, people diagnosed with bipolar disorder report a number of positive experiences associated with changes in their moods, such as increased sensitivity and alertness, higher productivity, being more comfortable and outgoing in social situations, increased sexual enjoyment, and heightened creativity (Jamison et al. 1980). In fact, people with bipolar disorder are more likely to pursue creative occupations than others are (Tremblay, Grosskopf, and Yang 2010). The reasons why creativity is more common among people with bipolar disorder aren't fully understood, but for many, this is one of the silver linings of the disorder.

Bipolar disorder is also related to the drive for success, and those with the disorder tend to have higher ambition and confidence about accomplishing difficult goals, particularly when experiencing positive moods (Johnson 2005b). Perhaps the genes for this disorder are in some way tied to the biological underpinnings of accomplishment. For instance, family members of people with bipolar disorder tend to experience high levels of success in both creative and career pursuits (Johnson 2005b).

Gaining control over manic symptoms may help these positive tendencies shine through. There is evidence that the milder mania symptoms are, the greater the degree of accomplishment in creative and other endeavors. And for those who do go through manic episodes, quelling the most severe symptoms can help them achieve more creative and professional success. To state it more bluntly, symptoms of mania such as anger, hypersexuality, and poor judgment may inhibit creativity and productivity. Therefore, building a plan for wellness may provide the additional benefit of helping you meet your career goals and be more creative.

MAINTAINING PERSPECTIVE AND SELF-ACCEPTANCE

Remember that having a diagnosis of bipolar disorder does not define you. You are a person with bipolar disorder, not a bipolar person. While having this condition requires that you monitor your moods and receive lifetime treatment, you can still live a rich and fulfilling life. Each step you take toward extending periods of wellness will increase your self-awareness, help you recognize your strengths, and allow you to learn from your challenges.

There may be times during a manic or depressive episode when you think or act in ways that aren't consistent with your personal goals or values. It can be easy to feel bad about yourself in the aftermath. Having self-compassion as you pick up the pieces and get back on track can be as important as any of the other strategies discussed in this book. Being willing to forgive yourself and learning to use challenges and barriers as opportunities for growth are important steps on the path to wellness.

CLOSING THOUGHTS

We believe the key to staying healthy is learning as much as possible about bipolar disorder and strategies you can use to prolong periods of balanced mood. You may recall that this type of learning is called psychoeducation, and in a sense, reading this book was like taking a mini psychoeducation course. We wrote this book with the goal of helping you learn more about your illness and empowering you to maximize your periods of wellness. We congratulate you on finishing it! You have taken a meaningful step toward building a plan for wellness.

You now know how doctors diagnose bipolar disorder, how to identify symptoms of depression and mania, and how to find professional help and choose the services and treatment team that are best for you. You're familiar with the types of medications commonly prescribed to treat bipolar disorder and the psychosocial treatments that can help you stay well. You have learned how to identify your personal triggers and warning signs and why doing so is important. You've learned strategies for responding to or managing triggers and warning signs so you can minimize symptoms when they occur. You've spent some time thinking about factors that may influence whether you disclose your illness to others and how you might talk with them about your illness. Finally, you've considered some of the benefits of receiving a diagnosis and some of the positive aspects of the illness. Armed with all of this information, you have tools for helping ensure your well-being and good reason to feel hopeful about the future.

We hope this book continues to serve as a useful resource when you're looking for information about what it means to have bipolar disorder, strategies to manage your symptoms, or ideas on how to extend periods of wellness. Although we have just summed up the contents of this book in a few sentences, you've gained a great deal of understanding, along with many helpful strategies for staying well, by reading these eight brief chapters. You are now knowledgeable about bipolar disorder and, of course, an expert in your own experience. We wish you the best, and we thank you for allowing us to be part of your journey toward wellness.

RESOURCES

SELF-HELP BOOKS

Basco, M. R., *The Bipolar Workbook: Tools for Controlling Your Mood Swings*

Burns, D. M., *Feeling Good: The New Mood Therapy*

Fast, J., and J. Preston, *Loving Someone with Bipolar Disorder*

Jones, S., P. Hayward, and D. Lam, *Coping with Bipolar Disorder: A CBT-Informed Guide to Living with Manic Depression*

Last, C. G., *When Someone You Love Is Bipolar: Help and Support for You and Your Partner*

Miklowitz, D., *The Bipolar Survival Guide*

Otto, M., and A. Henin, *Living with Bipolar Disorder*

Otto, M., N. Reilly-Harrington, R. O. Knauz, A. Henin, J. N. Kogan, and G. S. Sachs, *Managing Bipolar Disorder: A Cognitive Behavioral Treatment Program Workbook*

Paterson, R., *Your Depression Map: Find the Source of Your Depression and Chart Your Recovery.*

Phelps, J. R., *Why Am I Still Depressed? Recognizing and Managing the Ups and Downs of Bipolar II and Soft Bipolar Disorder*

Torrey, E. F., and M. B. Knable, *Surviving Manic-Depression: A Manual on Bipolar Disorder for Patients, Families, and Providers*

AUTOBIOGRAPHIES AND NONFICTION ACCOUNTS

Gibbons, K., *Sights Unseen*

Solomon, A., *The Noonday Demon: An Atlas of Depression*

Styron, W., *Darkness Visible: A Memoir of Madness*

Jamison, K. R., *An Unquiet Mind: A Memoir of Moods and Madness*

Jamison, K. R., *Night Falls Fast: Understanding Suicide*

Jamison, K. R., *Touched with Fire: Manic-Depressive Illness and the Artistic Temperament*

CHILDREN'S BOOKS

Chan, P. D., *Why is Mommy Sad? A Child's Guide to Parental Depression*

Holloway, A., *The Bipolar Bear Family: When a Parent Has Bipolar Disorder*

PUBLISHERS AND MAGAZINES

New Harbinger Publications: newharbinger.com (books on depression, bipolar disorder, anxiety, and more)

bp Magazine: bphope.com ("hope and harmony for people with bipolar")

Esperanza Magazine: www.hopetocope.com ("hope to cope with anxiety and depression")

INFORMATION ON TREATMENTS, MEDICATIONS, AND REFERRALS

American Psychological Association: locator.apa.org

Association for Behavioral and Cognitive Therapies: abct.org

Depression and Bipolar Support Alliance: findapro.dbsapages.org

National Network of Depression Centers: www.nndc.org /centers-of-excellence

ORGANIZATIONS AND GENERAL INFORMATION

Brain and Behavior Research Foundation: bbrfoundation.org

Depression and Bipolar Support Alliance: www.dbsalliance.org

Facing Us: www.facingus.org (various wellness tools and resources)

International Foundation for Research and Education on Depression: ifred.org

National Alliance on Mental Illness: nami.org (consumer and family support groups)

National Institute of Mental Health: www.nimh.nih.gov/health /publications/bipolar-disorder/complete-index.shtml

The Sean Costello Memorial Fund for Bipolar Disorder Research: www.seancostellofund.org

Substance Abuse and Mental Health Services Administration: www.samhsa.gov

U.S. Equal Employment Opportunity Commission: eeoc.gov

ONLINE TOOLS

Finance management: www.hellowallet.com

Life charting: bipolarnews.org/?page_id=175

Mood Tracking

https://moodtracker.com

www.moodscope.com

www.facingus.org/tour/tracker

Mood, sleep, and exercise tracking: www.medhelp.org

Sleep diary: type "National Sleep Foundation sleep diary" into an Internet search engine

Wellness planning: www.facingus.org/tour/plan

Personal Testimonials

www.victoriamaxwell.com

www.youtube.com/user/DBSAlliance

REFERENCES

Altshuler, L. L., R. M. Post, G. Hellemann, G. S. Leverich, W. A. Nolen, M. A. Frye, P. E. Keck, R. W. Kupka, H. Grunze, S. L. McElroy, C. A. Sugar, and T. Suppes. 2009. Impact of antidepressant continuation after acute positive or partial treatment response for bipolar depression: A blinded, randomized study. *Journal of Clinical Psychiatry* 70:450-457.

American Psychiatric Association. 2002. APA Practice Guidelines: Treatment of Patients with Bipolar Disorder, Second Edition. Psychiatry Online, DOI: 10.1176/ appi.books .9780890423363.50051. Downloaded from http://psychiatry online.org/content.aspx?bookid=28&#0022;sectionid =1669577#50051.

Barbini, B., C. Colombo, F. Benedetti, E. Campori, L. Bellodi, and E. Smeraldi. 1998. The unipolar-bipolar dichotomy and the response to sleep deprivation. *Psychiatry Research* 79:43-50.

Basco, M. R. 2006. *The Bipolar Workbook: Tools for Controlling Your Mood Swings.* New York: Guilford Press.

Beck, A. T. 1964. Thinking and depression: II. Theory and Therapy. *Archives of General Psychiatry* 10:561-571.

Chen, Y. W., and S. C. Dilsaver. 1996. Lifetime rates of suicide attempts among subjects with bipolar and unipolar disorders relative to subjects with other axis I disorders. *Biological Psychiatry* 39:896-899.

Chengappa, K. N. R., J. Levine, D. Rathore, H. Parepally, and R. Atzert. 2001. Long-term effects of topiramate on bipolar mood instability, weight change, and glycemic control: A case-series. *European Psychiatry* 16:186-190.

Colom, F., and E. Vieta. 2006. *Psychoeducation Manual for Bipolar Disorder.* Cambridge: Cambridge University Press.

Colombo, C., F. Benedetti, B. Barbini, E. Campori, and E. Smeraldi. 1999. Rate of switch from depression into mania after therapeutic sleep deprivation in bipolar depression. *Psychiatry Research* 86:267-270.

Coryell, W., C. Turvey, J. Endicott, A. C. Leon, T. Mueller, D. Solomon, and M. Keller. 1998. Bipolar I affective disorder:

Predictors of outcome after 15 years. *Journal of Affective Disorders* 50:109-116.

Cuellar, A. K., S. L. Johnson, and R. Winters. 2005. Distinctions between bipolar and unipolar depression. *Clinical Psychology Review* 25:307-339.

Dunn, A. L., M. H. Trivdei, J. B. Kampert, C. G. Clark, and H. O. Chambliss. 2005. Exercise treatment for depression: Efficacy and dose response. *American Journal of Preventive Medicine* 28:1-8.

Frank, E., D. J. Kupfer, M. E. Thase, A. G. Mallinger, H. A. Swartz, A. M. Fagiolini, V. Grochocinski, P. Houck, J. Scott, W. Thompson, and T. Monk. 2005. Two-year outcomes for interpersonal and social rhythm therapy in individuals with bipolar I disorder. *Archives of General Psychiatry* 62:996-1004.

Ghaemi, S. N., M. S. Lenox, and R. J. Baldessarini. 2001. Effectiveness and safety of long-term antidepressant treatment in bipolar disorder. *Journal of Clinical Psychiatry* 62:565-569.

Gitlin, M. J., J. Swendsen, T. L. Heller, and C. Hammen. 1995. Relapse and Impairment in Bipolar Disorder. *American Journal of Psychiatry* 152:1635-1640.

Gurling, H., C. Smyth, G. Kalsi, E. Moloney, L. Rifkin, J. O'Neill, P. Murphy, D. Curtis, H. Petursson, and J. Brynjolfsson. 1995. Linkage findings in bipolar disorder. *Nature Genetics* 8:291-296.

Hammen, C., M. Gitlin, and L. Altshuler. 2000. Predictors of work adjustment in bipolar I patients: A naturalistic longitudinal follow-up. *Journal of Consulting and Clinical Psychology* 68:220-225.

Harvey, A. G. 2008. Sleep and Circadian Rhythms in Bipolar Disorder: Seeking Synchrony, Harmony, and Regulation. *American Journal of Psychiatry* 165:820-829.

Harvey, A. G., L. S. Talbot, and A. Gershon. 2009. Sleep Disturbance in Bipolar Disorder across the Lifespan. *Clinical Psychology: Science and Practice* 16:256-277.

Jamison, K. R. 1993. *Touched with Fire: Manic-Depressive Illness and the Artistic Temperament.* New York: Free Press.

Jamison, K. J., R. H. Gerner, C. Hammen, and C. Padesky. 1980. Clouds and Silver Linings: Positive Experiences Associated with Primary Affective Disorders. *American Journal of Psychiatry* 137:198-202.

Johnson, S. L. 2005a. Life events in bipolar disorder: Towards more specific models. *Clinical Psychology Review* 25:1008-1027.

Johnson, S. L. 2005b. Mania and dysregulation in goal pursuit: A review. *Clinical Psychology Review* 25:241-262.

Johnson, S. L., A. K. Cuellar, C. Ruggero, C. Winett-Perlman, P. Goodnick, R. White, and I. Miller. 2008. Life events as predictors of mania and depression in bipolar I disorder. *Journal of Abnormal Psychology* 117:268-277.

Johnson, S. L., L. R. Eisner, and C. S. Carver. 2009. Elevated expectancies among persons diagnosed with bipolar disorders. *British Journal of Clinical Psychology* 48:217-222.

Johnson, S. L., G. Murray, B. Frederickson, E. Youngstrom, S. Hinshaw, J. M. Bass, T. Deckersbach, J. Schooler, and I. Salloum. 2012. Creativity and Bipolar Disorder: Touched by Fire or Burning with Questions? *Clinical Psychology Review* 32:1-12.

Khan, A., L. D. Ginsberg, G. M. Asnin, F. K. Goodwin, K. H. Davis, A. A. Krishnan, and B. E. Adams. 2004. Effect of lamotrigine on cognitive complaints in patients with bipolar I disorder. *Journal of Clinical Psychiatry* 65:1483-1490

Kupfer, D. J. 2005. The increasing medical burden in bipolar disorder. *Journal of the American Medical Association* 293:2528-2530.

Lam, D., and G. Wong. 1997. Prodromes, coping strategies, insight, and social functioning in bipolar affective disorders. *Psychological Medicine* 27:1091-1100.

McElroy, S. L., L. L. Altshuler, T. Suppes, P. E. Keck, M. A. Frye, K. D. Denikoff, W. A. Nolen, R. W. Kupka, G. S. Leverich, J. R. Rochussen, A. J. Rush, and R. M. Post. 2001. Axis I psychiatric comorbidity and its relationship to historical illness variables in 288 patients with bipolar disorder. *American Journal of Psychiatry* 158:420-426.

Merikangas, K. R., H. S. Akiskal, J. Angst, P. E. Greenberg, R. M. A. Hirschfeld, M. Petukhova, and R. C. Kessler. 2007.

Lifetime and 12-Month Prevalence of Bipolar Spectrum Disorder in the National Comorbidity Survey Replication. *Archives of General Psychiatry* 64:543-552.

Miklowitz, D. J., E. L. George, J. A. Richards, T. L. Simoneau, and R. L. Suddath. 2003. A randomized study of family-focused psychoeducation and pharmacotherapy in the outpatient management of bipolar disorder. *Archives of General Psychiatry* 60:904-912.

Miklowitz. D. J., M. W. Otto, E. Frank, N. A. Reilly-Harrington, S. R. Wisniewski, J. N. Kogan, A. A. Nierenberg, J. R. Calabrese, L. B. Marangell, L. Gyulai, M. Araga, J. M. Gonzalez, E. R. Shirley, M. E. Thase, and G. S. Sachs. 2007. Psychosocial treatments for bipolar depression: A 1-year randomized trial from the Systematic Treatment Enhancement Program. *Archives of General Psychiatry* 64:419-427.

National Institutes of Health. 2005. National Institutes of Health State of the Science Conference Statement on Manifestations and Management of Chronic Insomnia in Adults, June 13-15, 2005. *Sleep* 28:1049-1057.

Nierenberg, A. A, S. Miyahara, T. Spencer, S. R. Wisniewski, M. W. Otto, N. Simon, M. H. Pollack, M. J. Ostacher, L. Yan, R. Siegel, and G. S. Sachs. 2005. Clinical and diagnostic implications of lifetime attention-deficit/hyperactivity disorder comorbidity in adults with bipolar disorder: Data from the first 1000 STEP-BD participants. *Biological Psychiatry* 57:1467-1473.

Noaghiul, S., and J. R. Hibbeln. 2003. Cross-national comparisons of seafood consumption and rates of bipolar disorders. *American Journal of Psychiatry* 160:2222-2227.

Nurnberger, J. I., and T. Foroud. 2000. Genetics of bipolar affective disorder. *Current Psychiatry Reports* 2:147-157.

Ornoy, A. 2006. Neuroteratogens in man: An overview with special emphasis on the teratogenicity of antiepileptic drugs in pregnancy. *Reproductive Toxicology* 22:214-226.

Regier, D. A., M. E. Farmer, D. S. Rae, B. Z. Locke, S. J. Keith, L. L. Judd, and F. K. Goodwin. 1990. Comorbidity of mental disorders with alcohol and other drug abuse: Results from the Epidemiologic Catchment Area (ECA) Study. *Journal of the American Medical Association* 264:2511-2518.

Sachs, G. S., A. A. Nierenberg, J. R. Calabrese, L. B. Marangell, S. R. Wisniewski, L. Gyulai, E. Friedman, C. L. Bowden, M. D. Fossey, M. J. Ostacher, T. A. Ketter, J. Patel, P. Hauser, D. Rapport, J. M. Martinez, M. H. Allen, D. J. Miklowitz, M. W. Otto, E. B. Dennehy, and M. E. Thase. 2007. Effectiveness of adjunctive antidepressant treatment for bipolar depression. *New England Journal of Medicine* 35:1711-1722.

Sachs, G. S., L. G. Sylvia, and H. G. Lund. 2009. Pharmacological treatment of acute bipolar depression. In *Bipolar Depression: Molecular Neurobiology, Clinical Diagnosis, and Pharmacotherapy*. Basel, Switzerland: Birkhauser.

Scott, J. 2001. Cognitive therapy as an adjunct to medication in bipolar disorder. *British Journal of Psychiatry* 178:s164-s168.

Scott, J. 2002. Using health belief models to understand the efficacy-effectiveness gap for mood stabilizer treatments. *Neuropsychobiology* 46:13-15.

Simon, N. M., M. Otto, R. Weiss, M. S. Bauer, S. Miyahara, S. R. Wisniewski, M. E. Thase, J. Kogan, E. Frank, A. A. Nierenberg, J. R. Calabrese, G. S. Sachs, and M. H. Pollack. 2004. Pharmacotherapy for bipolar disorder and comorbid conditions: Baseline data from STEP-BD. *Journal of Clinical Psychopharmacology* 24:512-520.

Simoneau, T. L., D. J. Miklowitz, J. A. Richards, R. Saleem, G. Rakhshanda, and E. L. George. 1999. Bipolar disorder and family communication: Effects of a psychoeducational treatment program. *Journal of Abnormal Psychology* 108:588-597.

Tondo, L., and R. J. Baldessarini. 2000. Reduced suicide risk during lithium maintenance treatment. *Journal of Clinical Psychiatry* 61:97-104.

Tremblay, C. H., S. Grosskopf, and K. Yang. 2010. Brainstorm: Occupational choice, bipolar illness, and creativity. *Economics and Human Biology* 8:233-241.

Wilson, R. 2006. *Stephen Fry: The Secret Life of the Manic-Depressive* [DVD]. London, United Kingdom: IWC Media/ BBC Scotland

Janelle M. Caponigro, MA, is a doctoral student in clinical science at the University of California, Berkeley, specializing in the social and emotional functioning of individuals with bipolar disorder and schizophrenia. She helped design and lead a sixteen-week bipolar psychoeducation group.

Erica H. Lee, MA, is a doctoral student in clinical science at the University of California, Berkeley, specializing in the sociocultural and contextual mechanisms underlying child and adolescent development and family functioning. She helped design and lead a sixteen-week bipolar psychoeducation group.

Sheri L. Johnson, PhD, is professor of psychology at the University of California, Berkeley. Her work has focused on bipolar disorder, specifically, the processes that trigger manic relapse and how these can be more effectively treated. She has published over 130 articles and book chapters and has coauthored or coedited numerous books.

Ann M. Kring, PhD, is professor of psychology at the University of California, Berkeley. She has taught graduate and undergraduate courses in severe mental illness since 1991. She has published over eighty articles and book chapters, as well as five books.

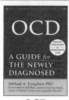

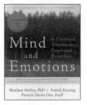